D0198300

ONE WEEK LOAN

Renew Books on PHONE-it: 1443 654456

Books are to be returned on or before the last date below

WINDSURFING

CROWOOD SPORTS GUIDES
WINDSURFING
TECHNIQUE•TACTICS•TRAINING

Penny Way

The Crowood Press

First published in 1991 by
The Crowood Press Ltd
Gipsy Lane, Swindon
Wiltshire SN2 6DQ

© The Crowood Press Ltd 1991

All rights reserved. No part of this publication may be reproduced or transmitted in
any form or by any means, electronic or mechanical, including photocopy, recording,
or any information storage and retrieval system, without permission in writing from
the publishers.

British Library Cataloguing in Publication Data

Way, Penny
    Windsurfing: technique, tactics, training – (Crowood sports guides series).
    1. Wind surfing
    I. Title
    797.33

ISBN 1 85223 481 4

Learning Resources
Centre

1104 1544

Acknowledgements

I would like to thank the following for supplying the equipment which enabled us to
take the photographs for this book: Fanatic/Art for supplying the boards and sails,
Typhoon International for supplying the wetsuits and Shorebreak designs for
supplying the harnesses.

Picture Credits

Photos by Richard Langdon/Ocean Images
Artwork by Taurus Graphics

Throughout this book the pronouns 'he', 'him' and 'his' have been used inclusively and
are intended to apply to both males and females.

Typeset by Chippendale Type Ltd., Otley, West Yorkshire.
Printed in Hong Kong by South China Printing Co.

CONTENTS

Preface   7

Part 1: Introduction to Windsurfing
  1 Starting Off   10
  2 Choosing a Board   13
  3 Choosing a Rig   17
  4 Buying a Second-Hand Board and Rig   20
  5 What to Wear   21
  6 How and Where to Learn   23

Part 2: Skills and Techniques
  7 Beginner's Techniques   26
  8 Intermediate Techniques   46
  9 Advanced Techniques   75
 10 Introduction to Competition   89

Part 3: Safety
 11 Safety for the Windsurfer   102
 12 Care of Equipment   108

Part 4: Fitness
 13 General Fitness   112
 14 Weight Training   115
 15 Specific Fitness Training for the Windsurfer   117
 16 Flexibility   118
 17 Injury Prevention   119
 18 Mental Training and the Inner Game   120

     Appendix   123
     Glossary   124
     Index   126

PREFACE

When I was learning to windsurf I could not afford windsurfing lessons as I was a student. I borrowed a book from the library, and armed with this and my second-hand board, I would go and sail from a beach I knew was going to be used for lessons that day. I watched the instructor and the class and then gave it a go. My first attempts were wet but I persevered. I got very tired but I loved it and met some very friendly people. I was hooked – all I could talk about was windsurfing and things haven't changed ten years on!

When I was learning, I was lucky that the instructor on whom I eavesdropped was sympathetic to my situation – he gave me tips and suggested ways I could practise to get over the inevitable hurdles. I recommend that anyone wanting to learn to windsurf takes lessons, as they will save a lot of time in the future and provide a safe environment to start from – you can even do the course in just one day. However, a good book to refer to before, during and after lessons will help you immensely.

Throughout this book I have suggested exercises similar to those I used when learning and I have also listed the key points of each important manoeuvre. You will find that if you can master the key points correctly the rest will come naturally.

Good luck, and I hope that you get as much fun from windsurfing as I have!

Fig 1   Course racing boards on a fast reaching leg.

PART I

INTRODUCTION TO WINDSURFING

CHAPTER I

STARTING OFF

Many people have claimed that they invented the windsurfer since the sport became so popular, but the first time a board and sail appeared on the water in a form that we would recognize as today's windsurfer was in the late 1960s in California. It was used by Hoyle Schweitzer and Jim Drake who patented the Windsurfer in 1968. They had both been sailors and surfers and were looking for a way of combining the best of both sports. They succeeded with their original windsurfer which consisted of an ordinary surfboard and a triangular sail attached to the board by a universal joint – this allowed the rig to be moved in any direction.

Since its invention in 1968 the windsurfer has been refined so that it is easier to use in all conditions, but the basic idea remains the same. As more people were introduced to the sport by Hoyle and his family the sport grew rapidly and spread across America. Eventually it spread to the shores of Europe where it grew in epidemic proportions. The windsurfer lent itself ideally to racing, and weekend races were organised for anyone interested. This interest grew phenomenally across the world and European and World Championships were soon being organised with over 500 competitors from every corner of the globe attending.

Windsurfing was and still is a sport for people of all ages and physiques. Whether you are 8 or 88 you are never too young to learn! All you need is to be able to swim 25m (25yd) and have a reasonable level of health. Windsurfing is a very easy sport to enjoy – it is simple to prepare for, it is easy to put the board and rig together on the beach and it doesn't cost a great deal once you have the basics.

Whether you are learning to windsurf for fun during your summer holiday or hope to become a pro-racer or Olympic champion you will certainly enjoy yourself.

Beginner's Board and Rig

Fig 2 shows the different parts of equipment used. As you progress through this book these different parts will be referred to, so an explanation of the components is given overleaf. Also, for an

Fig 2   A beginner's board and rig.

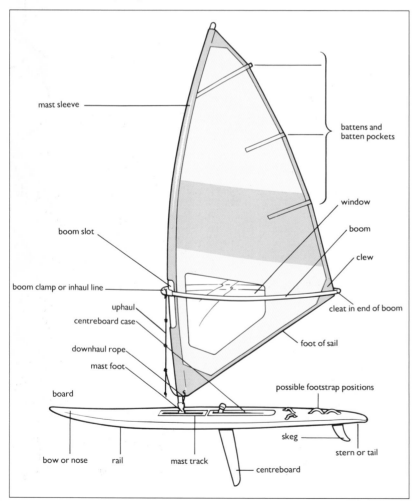

- mast sleeve
- battens and batten pockets
- window
- boom
- clew
- cleat in end of boom
- foot of sail
- boom slot
- boom clamp or inhaul line
- uphaul
- centreboard case
- downhaul rope
- mast foot
- board
- possible footstrap positions
- skeg
- stern or tail
- bow or nose
- rail
- mast track
- centreboard

Fig 3   Christine Lapworth racing her one design Mistral.

explanation of the wind speed values used in this book, please see the Appendix.

Batten – fibreglass strips that help control the shape of the sail.

Batten pocket – the pocket into which the batten fits.

Board – the main structure on which you stand – it is normally made out of polyethylene, various composites of fibres and polyester or epoxy resins and foam.

Bow – the front of the board.

Boom – the aluminium bar that encompasses the sail and attaches to the mast and clew of the sail – it is normally coated with a rubber grip. Booms are used for steering from either side of the sail and should be set at about shoulder height.

Boom slot – the cut out in the luff tube of the sail where the boom attaches to the mast.

Boom clamp – the clamp that connects the boom to the mast.

Clew – the back corner of the sail.

Cleat – a system for holding a piece of rope in place.

Centreboard – the centreboard is normally made of plastic or glass fibre and is positioned in the centre of the board behind the mast track. Most centreboards are fully retracting. They are used fully down in light winds and are retracted in shallow water and windy conditions – *see* the following chapters.

Centreboard case – the case into which the centreboard fits. This is built into the board.

Downhaul – the rope that controls the tension of the front of the sail. It connects the tack of the sail to the mast foot.

Foot – the bottom edge of the sail.

Footstraps – these are fitted to most boards and are normally made of plastic and neoprene and can be adjusted to fit the size of your feet. They help to hold your feet on the board when you are travelling at speed and over waves.

Inhaul – the rope that is sometimes used to connect the boom to the mast instead of a clamp.

Mast – the mast is a tapered fibreglass or aluminium tube that slides up inside the sail.

Mast sleeve – the sleeve of the sail into which the mast fits.

Mast extension – if the mast needs to be extended to fit a different sail an extension is used. This slots into the base of the mast and is made of aluminium or carbon. Mast extensions are normally adjustable in length.

Mast foot – the part that connects the mast to the board. It consists of a universal joint that enables the mast and sail to be turned and inclined in any direction.

Mast socket or *track* – some boards just have a single socket into which the mast foot fits. Other boards have a mast track that enables the position of the mast socket to be moved up and down the board.

Nose – another term for the front of the board.

Rail – the edge of the board.

Skeg – the skeg helps the steering of the board and is made of plastic, fibreglass or carbon fibre. It is very stiff and fits into the skeg box on the under-surface of the board near the stern.

Skeg box – this is built into the board and holds the skeg in place.

Stern – the back of the board.

Tail – another term for the back of the board.

Uphaul – the rope used to pull the sail out of the water. One end is attached to the front of the boom, the other is free but elasticated away to the mast base. The uphaul normally consists of a thick rope with knots tied in it to make it easy to grip. Sometimes it has elastic built into it rather than tied to it.

Window – most sails have a clear panel which allows good visibility so that you can see other sailors and obstacles.

Fig 4   Boards, rigs and competitors waiting for the start of racing.

CHAPTER 2

CHOOSING A BOARD

In the early days there was only one type of board and one sail that everybody used in all weather conditions, whether you were beginner or expert. This certainly saved a lot of money but made learning and progressing an uphill struggle except for the most dedicated enthusiasts!

Equipment and development have come a long way since 1968; boards are now a lot lighter and easier to manage in and out of the water. The sails, mast and booms are also much easier to use and control in a greater wind range as they are lighter and stiffer.

There is now different equipment manufactured for the different levels and interests of the windsurfer and for different wind conditions. There are boards for beginners, intermediates and advanced windsurfers and there are also special boards for racing, speed sailing, slalom racing, wave jumping and riding. Likewise there are special rigs for beginners, advanced sailors and racers.

I will try to guide you through this variety of choice in the following pages. The board and rig can be split into two separate components, and the rig is dealt with in the next chapter.

Boards

If you walk into a windsurfing shop or glance through a magazine you will be struck by the vast number of boards there are to choose from. Up until now you probably thought a board was a board, but this is not true as not all windsurfers are the same. Boards vary in four main areas: volume; weight; size; and construction. Volume is the most important difference so let us start with that.

Volume

The volume of a board is equal to the amount of filling it contains. It is measured in litres and is calculated by measuring the amount of water that is displaced when the board is totally immersed. Most manufacturers advertise the volume of their boards in their brochures. It is vital that you know what board volume is suitable for you – the heavier you are the more volume you will need and the lighter you are, the less volume is necessary. The more volume a board has, the more stable it is in light winds. However, as the wind increases, high-volume boards become hard to sail as they tend to fly out of the water – their large surface area is exposed to the wind. Now you will begin to understand why so many different boards are necessary for different abilities and different weather conditions.

Weight

As you examine different boards you will realize that some boards are a lot lighter than others even though they look to be the same size. This difference in weight will also probably be indicated by the price tag! The lighter boards tend to be more expensive because more expensive materials have been used in their construction. The advantages of a light board are that it is faster than a heavier board of the same design and is easier to lift and carry off the water. However, heavier boards are often more durable and better suited to the beginner or recreational windsurfer who wants to throw his or her board around the beach without having to worry about it! A heavy board weighs 18–20kg (40–44lb). A light board can weigh as little as 7kg (15.5lb) depending on its size.

Construction

Different construction methods and materials are used for different boards. Most boards are solid and are made from two main components: the skin and the core. Boards are strengthened with stringers to prevent breakage. The main types of skin used are polyethylene and various composites of fibres and polyester or epoxy resins coated with a plastic.

Polyethylene is a type of plastic and is the most common material used for boards at the cheaper end of the market. This is primarily because it is a cheap material to use. However, polyethylene boards are ideal for the beginner and recreational sailor because the plastic is so durable. Polyethylene is not used in racing boards because it is too heavy and flexible compared with the more expensive materials that are available.

The composite skins are generally lighter than polyethylene but need to be looked after because they are not as durable. They are also more expensive to work with.

There are two different sorts of foam that are used for the core; these are polyurethane and polystyrene. Generally the cheaper boards are made with a polyurethane core which is less expensive to work with, but it results in a heavier board. Polystyrene is used in the majority of production racing boards because it is lighter. A higher level of technology is needed when working with polystyrene so the end product is usually more expensive.

Size

Boards vary in size depending on the purpose for which they have been designed. The biggest boards (340–390cm,

134–153.5in) perform best in light winds and are ideal for beginners or as light wind racing boards, although they can be used by windsurfers of any standard when the wind is light.

Boards that are between 300cm (118in) and 340cm (134in) long have been designed for higher wind use. Due to their small size they are unstable when used in winds under force 3 and so are not suitable for beginners who need to learn in light winds. A board of this size is ideal for the intermediate windsurfer who is learning to master strong wind techniques, as it is more manoeuvrable than the beginner's board once the wind picks up. It is also a good size for a very light person to learn on – those under 50kg (110lb), perhaps a child or slight woman.

Boards that are under 300cm (118in) long are purely for high wind use (force 4 and above). Depending on your weight and the volume of the board, you may be able to uphaul a board of this size, but if you can't you need to know how to waterstart! As boards decrease in size they become a lot more manoeuvrable in extreme conditions, but they need more wind if you are to get the best out of them.

Now that you understand what the differences between the available boards are, below is a description and photograph (Fig 5) of each of the three main types of board – beginner's, intermediate's and advanced.

Fig 5   From right to left: a Fanatic 370 which is a beginner's board, a Fanatic 320 for intermediates and an advanced wave board.

A Beginner's or Light Wind Board

This is suitable for use by a beginner in force 1–3 winds.

Depending on the size of the beginner, a beginner's board should have at least 200 litres of volume. If it has insufficient volume it will be very unstable to learn on. It should be between 340–390cm (134–153.5in) long and again if the beginner is very small the board can be smaller. The board needs to have a large centreboard as this helps both stability and upwind performance. It is important that the centreboard is fully retracting – in other words that it disappears totally inside the

board when it is pushed back. As a beginner you don't necessarily need a mast track, and if your board does have one, lock the mast foot so that it is secured in the centre position and cannot move around. Some beginner's boards just have a single mast socket position which is adequate at this stage but it may limit your progress once you begin to sail in stronger winds.

A beginner's board does not need footstraps on it and these get in the way when you are learning. If your board does

have them, they are easily removed with a screwdriver. Keep them in a safe place until you have progressed to stronger wind techniques. When buying a beginner's board it is worthwhile getting one on to which you can fit footstraps in the future.

An Intermediate's or Medium Wind Board

This is suitable for use by intermediates in force 3–5 winds.

Fig 6 Nathalie Le Lievre, Funboard World Champion gybing in a course race.

An intermediate board is smaller than a beginner's board. It can be between 300cm (118in) and 340cm (134in) long. Because it is smaller it has less volume and is therefore easier to control in stronger winds. It has a fully retracting centreboard, but this can be smaller than those you find on a beginner's board as intermediates don't need as much stability. You need to be able to move the position of the mast foot on this type of board, so you need to have a sliding mast track. There should be at least six footstraps for two reaching positions.

An Advanced or High Wind Board

This is suitable for use by the advanced sailor in force 5 winds or more.

Advanced boards are all less than 300cm (118in) long. They are purely for the advanced sailor because they can only be sailed properly in strong winds. These boards do not have centreboards and rely solely on the skeg to help them sail upwind. The smaller the board the easier it is to sail in stronger winds. However, if you try and sail a board which is too small for your weight you will find it very difficult to trim properly and will only be able to enjoy yourself when it is very windy. The most advanced boards need to be waterstarted; they can not be uphauled easily because of their low volume. All advanced boards have at least three footstraps in the reaching position. Most have a fixed mast foot position which can be adjusted slightly off the water.

Calculating Board Volume

The importance of volume is seldom stressed enough. A board that is superb for you as an intermediate board may be totally inappropriate for somebody else of the same standard but of a different weight. The amount of volume you need in a board is totally dependent upon your weight. 1 litre of water weighs 1kg, therefore the flotation of a board is its volume minus its weight plus the weight of everything on it including the rig and sailor. You will also need reserve buoyancy to help you float higher and make the board more stable. To work out the amount of volume you need in a board, you must know:

1.   The weight of the board in kilograms.
2.   Your weight dressed in your wetsuit and harness in kilograms.
3.   The weight of the rig (approximately 9kg).
4.   The recommended reserve buoyancy for the type of board you are sailing, in other words beginner's, intermediate's or advanced.

Add these four figures together and the resultant figure will be the minimum amount of volume that you require for your weight on that type of board.

The recommended reserve buoyancy for a beginner's board is 110 litres; the more volume you have the more stable the board will be in light winds.

In an intermediate's board the recommended reserve buoyancy is a minimum of 40 litres. More volume will make the board more stable in light winds again, but it will be harder to manoeuvre when the wind picks up.

With an advanced board you do not need any reserve buoyancy unless you want to be able to uphaul or sail in very light winds. If you want to uphaul you need at least 15 litres of reserve buoyancy; if you just want to be able to float home when the wind dies you only need 3 litres. Many advanced sailors use boards with no reserve buoyancy in very strong winds and high waves – the less volume you have, the easier the boards are to control. However, they can appear very twitchy to the inexperienced and are impossible to uphaul – your waterstarting technique has to be perfect.

KIT CHECK

Make sure that you choose a board with adequate volume for your weight. If you try to learn on a board with too little volume it will be very unstable. To work out the amount of volume you need in a beginner's board add:

● The weight of the board (kg).
● Your weight plus the weight of your wetsuit and harness (kg).
● The weight of the rig (approximately 9kg).
● The reserve buoyancy for a beginner's board (this is 110 litres).

The total figure is the minimum amount of volume you will need.

CHAPTER 3

CHOOSING A RIG

Rig is the term used to describe the mast, boom and sail collectively. Different rigs are needed for different abilities. In Fig 7, three rigs are shown; one for beginners and intermediates; one for the advanced windsurfer; and one for the racer. Many different rigs are available today; the basics you need to look for to suit your windsurfing ability are given below.

The Beginner's and Intermediate's Rig

It is possible to use the same sail when learning as when progressing to intermediate techniques. If the beginner is very small there are specialist lightweight rigs, but these are normally discarded quickly for more powerful versions. The sail shown in Fig 7 has the option of a half- or full-length middle batten. The half-length batten is better for the beginner because it makes it easier to depower the sail. The full-length batten increases the power of the sail. When choosing your first rig the priorities are:

1. Light weight – this makes it easier to pull the rig out of the water and manoeuvre.
2. A boom length of approximately 2m (6.5ft) – any longer and it will be hard to pull out of the water, any shorter and the sail will feel very twitchy when you are learning.
3. Sail size, which depends on your weight. It should be between 4sq m (43 sq ft) and 6sq m (64.5 sq ft).

The Advanced Rig

When sailing in large waves or high winds you will find it easier to use a sail made

Fig 7 From left to right: a race rig, a beginner's or intermediate's rig and a wave rig.

especially for these conditions. As shown in Fig 7 the foot and clew are cut high so that the sail isn't hit by waves. The rig should have a short boom for the same reason and a closely-cut mast sleeve that cannot fill up with water and weigh you down when you are trying to waterstart. It is useful to have a dual batten system so that you can use the full-length battens in flat water and the half-length battens in rough water. (With these battens you can depower the sail for wave manoeuvres and the like.) It is important to use very strong masts and booms when sailing in waves. Do not use aluminium masts as these will bend permanently when caught in the shore break!

The Racing Rig

All racing rigs used in slalom, speed and course racing competitions are made with camber inducers. A camber inducer is a fitting that is attached to the batten at the mast end which then slots on to the mast. The camber inducer holds the battens rigidly in place, making the sail more stable. It rotates around the mast when the sail is tacked or gybed. These are not good sails for beginners as the camber inducers and wide luff sleeve add weight to the sail. The sails are also hard to depower.

The Rig Components

As mentioned previously, the rig consists of three components: the mast, sail and boom. It is important to match these three together to create a good rig. For this you need some information about the various differences you may come across.

Masts

It is best to use the type of mast that is recommended for your sail. If you use the wrong mast your sail can be hard to control because different masts have different degrees of stiffness and different bend characteristics. The degree of mast stiffness and bend type you need should be marked on your sail.

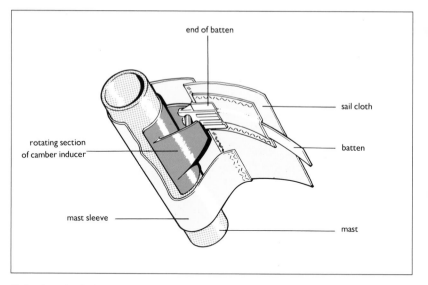

Fig 8   A camber inducer.

Most masts are tapered and made from epoxy, or epoxy and carbon if stiffness is a priority. Masts come in varying lengths, from 430–485cm (169–191in). If you need to lengthen a mast, mast extensions can be fitted and most sails have adjustable heads so that they can be lengthened to fit the mast if necessary. However, try and buy a mast which is the right length to fit your sails. Masts come in one or two pieces;

two-piece masts are easier to travel with as they do not overhang your car and they fit better into aircraft holds.

Booms

Booms are normally made from aluminium with plastic or aluminium ends, and are covered with a black rubber grip. The main difference between available

Fig 9   The boom clamp system.

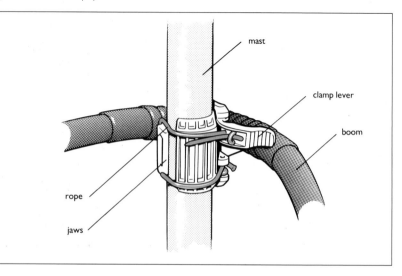

booms is their front-end fitting where they attach on to the mast. The original method of attaching the boom to the mast was to tie it on – this was complicated, time-consuming and normally inefficient. The latest generation of booms clamp on to the mast with the kind of fitting shown in Fig 9. This is a lot easier to use and ensures a firm fit every time. Most booms are adjustable and will say on them what their minimum or maximum length is. Try and buy one boom that will fit all your sails.

Wind force	1	2	3	4	5	6	7
Beginner's board	6.0	5.0	5.0				
Intermediate's board		6.5	6.0	5.5	5.0	4.5	
Advanced board				6.0	5.5	5.0	4.5

Sails

You will notice that sails are available in different sizes and materials. Different sized sails are used in different wind strengths and generally on a bigger board you will not need to use as small a sail as someone on a very tiny board. However, as a beginner you should not try sailing with too large a sail. Above is a chart showing the approximate sail size that should be used with each type of board in wind strengths varying from force 1–7.

This chart has been compiled for an average-sized person; if you are not average you will need to adjust the sizes accordingly. Obviously as you improve as a beginner, you can go out in lighter winds with a bigger sail and in stronger winds with a smaller sail. If you can only afford one or two sails, choose compromise sails that are neither too big nor too small.

Sail Materials

There are basically three main types of sail material which have been used in the manufacture of windsurfing sails. These are woven polyester, mylar and monofilm. Do not be confused by the fact that these basic materials are often found under different trade names in the sail manufacturers' brochures.

The original windsurfer sails were made of a woven polyester yarn which was very durable but which stretched with use so that sails often had to be replaced if they were to remain competitive.

As the sport developed, sail makers progressed to a material which was a combination of the original woven cloth and a plastic film. Sails made from this material, which was commonly known as mylar, had much better stretch characteristics than the original material. This is the material most commonly used today for beginners' and recreational windsurfers' sails.

The latest development in sails has been the use of monofilm. This is a totally clear plastic film – similar to that used in mylar but without the cloth. Monofilm has the advantage over previous materials in that it does not stretch in any direction and does not absorb water. Sails made out of this material are therefore very stable and light when in use. However, monofilm has to be looked after carefully as it can easily tear, so it is not suitable for the beginner who will often fall into the sail. Most race and high performance sails are now made out of monofilm.

Fig 10   The line start of a Mistral one design event.

CHAPTER 4

BUYING A SECOND-HAND BOARD AND RIG

If you are buying second-hand windsurfing gear you may well be able to pick up a bargain. There again, if you don't know what to look out for, you might not! Having said that, second-hand windsurfing equipment is normally excellent value for money. The best places to look for second-hand gear are the 'For Sale' sections of the windsurfing magazines or at your local club or windsurfing shop. When you go to look at a second-hand board, take an experienced windsurfer with you and bear the following points in mind:

1. Has the board got all the features you need, for example, sliding mast track and footstraps? If it hasn't it will be adequate for you to learn on but you will have to sell it to progress. If it is a real bargain it will be worthwhile buying it and then selling it to another beginner once you have progressed.
2. How heavy is it? If a board is very heavy it is often a sign that it has begun to delaminate and take on water. Delamination is when the fibres of the board begin to break down due to poor construction or a bad repair.
3. Check that all repairs are sound – if they are not the board may be prone to future leaks.
4. Check the mast for any cracks, especially around the base or where the boom attaches. A cracked mast will break, probably at the most inappropriate of moments. If it is an aluminium mast, make sure that it is straight. Masts that have been bent distort the sail shape when rigged up.
5. Make sure that the boom is the right

Fig 11   Barry Edgington competing in a course racing competition.

length for the sail and is neither extremely wide nor narrow. (Some earlier booms were funny shapes!) Make sure that the boom is not bent and that neither end is cracked. It is an idea to flex the boom to see how stiff it is – ideally you need a boom that is as stiff as possible.

6. Unroll the sail and check it for any tears. Make sure that it has all of its battens and fits properly on the mast and boom.

If everything is fine then buy it. As I mentioned previously, there are always many good bargains around.

CHAPTER 5

WHAT TO WEAR

From the first time that you stand on a board it is important that you wear protective clothing; whether you are in the tropics or cool areas you will need to protect yourself from the cold or sun.

The number one danger to windsurfers is the cold as exposure to cold water and wind when not properly prepared can cause hypothermia. In cold waters body temperature drops dramatically and the hypothermia process sets in. Even in

---

KIT CHECK

When sailing in cold weather always overdress because it will be a lot colder on the water than on land. Make sure your wetsuit fits well – it should be tight but not restricting. If it is too loose it will not be warm, but make sure that you have plenty of room for arm muscles. Wear shoes or boots to improve your grip on the board and protect your feet.

---

summer conditions this can happen – as soon as the water temperature drops below 20°C (68°F) (most of the year in many places) hypothermia can take effect.

The symptoms to look out for are: blue lips, apathy and tiredness followed by cramp, exhaustion and eventual collapse. To prevent hypothermia you need to wear a wetsuit.

Wetsuits

Wetsuits are close-fitting suits made of neoprene. They are worn over swimwear with no additional clothes underneath. In a conventional wetsuit some water gets inside but the suit remains warm if it fits

tightly enough. New-style wetsuits are now being made with dry zips and neoprene seals to prevent any water getting inside – these are a lot warmer for winter use.

Wetsuits come in different styles and thicknesses for the different seasons. Here are some of the different variations.

Fig 12   From left to right: drysuit, winter steamer, summer suit, summer shortie, drysuit boots, summer shoes, buoyancy aid, hat and gloves.

The Winter Steamer

These are made of 4–5mm (0.16–0.2in) thick neoprene and have full-length arms and legs. The body and legs should be tight fitting but with plenty of room to move in the shoulders and arms.

Drysuit

Also used in winter, these used to be a lot more popular than they are today. They are made from a lightweight breathable nylon material with drysuit seals, making a totally watertight suit. They are loose fitting with room for thermal clothing to be worn underneath. These are very warm suits, however, their drawback is that they are not very easy to swim or waterstart in.

The Summer Steamer

In warmer weather you will overheat in a winter steamer and so a cooler version is needed. Summer steamers are normally made of a lighter weight neoprene approximately 3mm (0.19in) thick. They work on the same principle as the winter steamer with some suits also having dry zips and good seals to minimise water entry. Most summer suits have short arms with the option of attaching longer arms for colder conditions.

The Shorty

In very warm weather you will want to wear a suit which has short legs as well as short arms – this is called a 'shorty'. These are normally made of neoprene of the same thickness as the summer steamer.

Footwear

Wetsuit Boots

In the colder months it is important to have good boots that keep your feet warm and have good grip and flexibility. It is very easy to tear a muscle in your ankles or feet if they are cold.

Summer Shoes

Many people sail in bare feet in the warmer months but if you are launching from a rocky shore, have sensitive feet or have a slippery board you will find summer shoes essential.

Head Gear

In cold weather more than 30 per cent of your body heat is lost through your head. A neoprene hat or helmet will keep you warm but when buying one make sure that it doesn't cover your ears as this will affect your balance.

Gloves

Hands get very cold in winter and many available gloves keep your hands warm but make it impossible to hang on to the boom without getting cramp. The best type of gloves to buy are drysuit gloves that are made out of a thin rubber similar to washing-up gloves. These are sealed at the wrist by fitting tightly under your wetsuit. Thin cotton inner gloves are worn underneath these to give you a bit more warmth. If you just want gloves to protect your hands and not keep them warm, you can use the short-fingered gloves that are

available with leather palms and breathable nylon backs which are very comfortable and unrestricting.

Avoiding the Sun

As the sun reflects back from the water it is easy to get too much exposure and this may cause problems. If you are not wearing a wetsuit you will need to protect your exposed skin with a good, non-greasy, waterproof sunblock. If you use a greasy sunblock, be careful that it doesn't get on to your board or boom to make them slippery. Use a hat to protect the top of your head and sunglasses or a visor to protect your eyes. Places to watch out for sunburn are the top of your shoulders and top of your feet – they are directly in line with the sun.

Buoyancy Aid

When you are learning or sailing on your own it is important to wear a buoyancy aid. There is some buoyancy in a wetsuit, but a buoyancy aid will also help you to float if you have an accident. You will find that a buoyancy aid is also useful when you are learning to waterstart.

Watch

You will probably need to tell the time when you are out windsurfing, whether it is so that you know when to put more money in the car park meter, or how long you have until the start of the next race. Use a waterproof and shockproof watch with a large read-out and easy-to-press stop-watch buttons.

CHAPTER 6

HOW AND WHERE TO LEARN

Learning successfully is dependent upon your first impressions of windsurfing. If you have a good first day you will more than likely love the sport, but if you have a bad one you will probably give up and vow never to try again. Whether you have a good or a bad first day depends on the wind and water conditions and your instructor. It is possible to learn solely from books but it is better to learn from an instructor and use a book purely as a guide before and after lessons and as you advance. It is generally not a good idea to learn from friends or relatives as you will probably end up falling out with each other!

> **STAR TIP**
>
> *I didn't take to it quickly because I didn't have any instruction. It took me about four weeks before I could even turn the board around.*
> Mark Woods
> *On Board*, 7(4), 1986.

It is best to learn at an official windsurfing school where they have special equipment for beginners, such as dry-land simulators, video facilities and rescue craft, not to mention qualified and experienced instructors. There are a

> **STAR TIP**
>
> *I would advise everyone who wants to improve to watch videos. Watch carefully, you can learn so much.*
> Mark Woods
> *On Board*, 7(4), 1986.

number of these schools around the country which have been approved by the Royal Yachting Association (RYA). They offer a standard beginners' course that can be completed in just one day. The cost for this is very reasonable. You can expect the course to consist of dry-land practice on a simulator followed by sessions on the water. Most schools provide their own wetsuits and buoyancy aids so all you need to take is yourself!

Learning Abroad

If you are planning to learn to windsurf during your holidays abroad make sure that you go to a proper windsurfing school where they have good equipment, speak English and have qualified instructors and rescue facilities. Often people try to learn from beach bums hiring boards off a beach who offer next to no instruction and who are often positioned in the worst place for

learning – crowded beaches with nasty shorebreaks and gusty winds. The RYA have a list of overseas schools that they have approved, so it is a good idea to contact them before leaving on your holidays.

Choose a day to learn yourself if you can. It is not worth having your first lesson on a rough sea with the wind blowing – you will just become quickly demoralized. Perfect conditions for learning are on flat water of a calm sea or lake. To find out where your nearest windsurfing school is, contact the sport's governing body or buy one of the windsurfing magazines.

In the following pages I explain the basic techniques you will be taught at your windsurfing lessons; use the book as a guide to recap and practise what you have been taught. Practice and time spent on the water are the keys to improving your windsurfing, so try the suggested exercises to perfect each technique and read the key points to make sure that you are not missing out on any vital pieces of information.

> **KEY POINT**
>
> Try to take your first lessons at an official windsurfing school where you can be guaranteed excellent instruction and facilities. You can start with a one-day course which is very reasonably priced.

PART 2
SKILLS AND TECHNIQUES

CHAPTER 7

BEGINNER'S TECHNIQUES

Selecting a Safe Launching Spot

Before you set sail as a beginner it is important that you choose a safe venue from which to launch. You may know of several popular windsurfing spots near you but these may only be suitable for the more advanced windsurfer rather than the beginner. Ask at your local windsurfing shop to find out the best place. It is a lot easier to learn the basics on a small lake or harbour rather than on the open sea. Ideally you want flat water, a force 2 wind and somewhere where you will not be in danger if you get tired – it is very easy to get carried away with the thrill when you are beginning.

As shown in Fig 13, a safe learning venue should have:

1. Cross- or onshore winds – if the wind is offshore it is dangerous to go out as you will be blown out to sea.

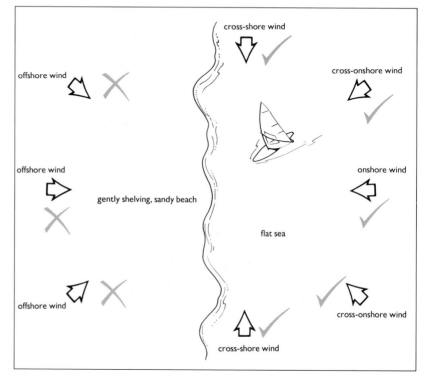

Fig 13   A safe learning venue.

> **RULES CHECK**
>
> Do not go out in offshore winds when you are learning as you will get blown out to sea.

2. Flat water which is a lot easier to balance on than rough water.
3. Safe and easy launching – not too many rocks or steep cliffs.
4. No strong tides or currents – find out about these from the locals. Strong tides can carry you off in a direction in which you don't want to go.
5. No hazards to hit such as crowds of swimmers; when you are learning it is easy to find yourself out of control.

> **RULES CHECK**
>
> Do not go out in strong tides as you may find it difficult to get back to the beach.

How to Tell Where the Wind is Coming From

When you are new to the sport it is often hard to tell where the wind is coming from even though everybody else seems to know instinctively. The best method I have found is to stand and turn around slowly until you can feel the wind coming directly square on to your face so that your hair is blowing straight back. You are now looking directly into the wind. It is very important to know always where the wind is coming from, and you should make a mental note of it each time you go out on the water.

> **RULES CHECK**
>
> Do not try to learn on a crowded beach where there are a lot of people swimming in the water – you may hit them if you find yourself out of control.

Fig 14   A one-handed jump – showing off to the crowds!

Figs 15 (a)–(g) Rigging up.

Fig 15 (a)   Sliding the mast into the sail until it reaches the head.

Fig 15 (b)   Thread the downhaul line through the bottom of the sail and back through the pulley system.

Fig 15 (c)   Attach the front of the boom to the mast at shoulder height.

Fig 15 (e)   Push against the end of the mast with your leg to help tension the downhaul line.

Fig 15 (f)   Put the battens into the batten pockets and tension the webbing.

Fig 15 (d)   Attach the clew of the sail to the end of the boom with the outhaul line.

Fig 15 (g)   Slacken the outhaul for a fuller sail; tighten it if you want it flatter.

Rigging Up *(Figs 15 (a)–(g))*

Once you have found a safe launching spot it is time to rig your sail up and put the board and rig together so that you can get started on the water. You may need to refer to Fig 1 which names all the parts of the rig. Rigging up is one of the most laborious of windsurfing tasks and I often wish that you could just push a button so that it would rig up automatically. Rigging up can be faster if you are organized and have previously made sure that masts, booms and bits of rope are all the right length for the sail you are using. I always label everything now to make my rigging up faster.

1.   Lay the mast, boom, sail, mast foot and battens out on a grassy area.
2.   Unroll the sail and slide the tapered end of the mast into the bottom of the sail luff tube until it reaches the top of the sail.
3.   Put the mast foot into the bottom of the mast and attach the downhaul line to the bottom of the sail and tension.
4.   Clamp or tie the boom on to the mast at shoulder height. You can either measure this with a tape measure or lie down against the mast on the grass.
5.   Attach the clew of the sail to the end of the boom either with a rope or rope and pulley and tension hard.
6.   Retension the downhaul – it will be easier now that there is more outhaul tension on the sail.
7.   Put the battens in.
8.   Let off the outhaul tension a fraction to put more fullness into the sail. If the sail is too flat it will have no power and will be hard to sail. However, if it is too full it will be hard to sail upwind.
9.   Attach the uphaul line to the mast base and make sure that all lines are secured.

The completed rig should now have a smooth aerofoil shape to it; if it does not, try retensioning the downhaul. Secure the rig so that it can't be blown by a gust of wind – to a tree or seat for example. If the rig is picked up by the wind it could be damaged, or even worse it could hit somebody and injure them.

Fig 16   Carry the board with one hand in the centreboard case and the other in the mast track.

Carrying the Board

Always carry the board to the water first. Before leaving your car make sure you have the centreboard in place and position it in the board so that it is not quite retracted – this gives you room to hold the board through the centreboard case.

Carry the board as in Fig 16 with one hand in the centreboard case and the other in the mast track.

KIT CHECK

However warm it is, always wear a full-length wetsuit when you are learning so that your legs have some protection against bruising if you fall off.

Fig 17   Practising balancing by kneeling on the board.

Fig 19   It is easiest in light winds to carry the rig above your head.

Balancing on the Board

This is a stage often missed out in the hurry to get up and going, but it is an important stage in getting your body used to balancing on the board.

Carry your board into thigh-deep water, put the centreboard down into its vertical position and try to climb on to the board and sit on it so that you are astride it. Once you have become used to this,

bring yourself up into a kneeling position, gain your balance and then slowly stand up.

Take your time and try and get used to the feeling of standing on the board. You will find that you have to use your arms to help balance yourself. Try walking towards the front of the board and then towards the back of the board, and then try to stand on just one leg! Don't worry if you have problems – it is a lot easier to balance on the board when you have a rig

to hold on to! Play around on the board until you become totally happy on it.

Once you have carried your rig to the water you are now ready to try the real thing!

Carrying the Rig

Carry the rig above your head as in Fig 19 with one hand on the mast and the other on the boom. Always have the mast at 90 degrees to the wind direction. (This is much easier to do when you are walking upwind.) When you are walking downwind it is easier to carry the rig if it is at waist level – again you should keep the mast at 90 degrees to the wind.

Attaching the Rig to the Board

Carry the rig into knee-deep water and then go back for the board. Put the board on its edge, put the mast foot into its

Fig 18   Standing on the board.

Fig 20   With the board on its edge, attach the rig to the board.

socket to attach the two together and then walk with them into thigh-deep water. Now it's time to try and get on to the board.

Getting on to the Board *(Figs 21 (a)–(c))*

1.   Once you are in thigh-deep water, make sure the centreboard is in its vertical position. Arrange the board and rig so that the wind is coming from behind you. The board should be at 90 degrees to the wind direction with the rig on the leeward side of the board. If you have a sliding mast track make sure that it is in a locked position with the mast foot on the centre position.

KEY POINT

Choose a safe venue from which to sail.

2.   Put your front hand on the centre of the board just in front of the mast foot and your back hand just in front of the centreboard case, also in the centre of the board.
3.   Push down on your hands and arms to pull your body on to the board so that you are kneeling on the centre-line of the board between your hands.

KEY POINT

Concentrate on keeping your weight over the centre-line of the board.

Figs 21 (a)–(c) Getting on to the board.

Fig 21 (a)   Position the board at 90 degrees to the wind, with the rig on the leeward side.

Fig 21 (b)   Put your front hand in front of the mast foot and your back hand just in front of the centreboard case.

Fig 21 (c)   Kneel between your hands over the centre-line of the board.

Pulling the Sail out of the Water *(Figs 22 (a)–(f))*

This is the hardest part of windsurfing for many people. It is very important to make your legs do all of the work and not your back.

1.   Starting from the kneeling position, take hold of the bottom of the uphaul line with one hand and use the other for balance.
2.   Bring your feet up underneath you so that you are in a crouching position.
3.   Straighten up into a standing position with your back straight and knees slightly bent. Your feet should both be pointing across the board, your front foot just in front of the mast and your back one just behind it but still over the centre-line of the board.
4.   By bending your legs (not your back) pull the rig partially clear of the surface so that the water drains from it – this will make the rig much lighter.
5.   Now bend your knees again and work hand over hand up the uphaul until the end of the boom is clear of the water. As soon as you can, move your hands from the uphaul to the mast, which is more stable.
6.   You should now be standing in a relaxed position with your arms and legs slightly bent. The rig and your body should form a V shape.

The rig should now be pointing directly downwind and flapping in front of you, and the board should be across the wind. This position is known as the 'secure position' because there is no power in the sail and the board cannot move off. This position will often be referred to later in the book. Before you start shooting off you must first learn how to turn around.

KEY POINT

Use your legs and not your back to pull the sail out of the water.

Figs 22 (a)–(f)   Pulling the sail out of the water.

Fig 22 (a)   Take hold of the bottom of the uphaul and balance yourself using your other hand.

Fig 22 (d)   Bend your knees and pull the rig partially clear of the water so that it drains.

Fig 22 (b)   Stand up into a crouched position with your feet taking the place of your knees.

Fig 22 (c)   Straighten up to the standing position with your back straight and knees slightly bent.

Fig 22 (e)   With your knees bent, work hand over hand up the uphaul line until the end of the boom is clear.

Fig 22 (f)   Take hold of the mast while standing with your arms and legs slightly bent – this is known as the secure position.

Figs 23 (a)–(d) Turning around on the spot.

Fig 23 (a) Lean the mast towards the back of the board and the nose will turn into the wind.

Fig 23 (b) Taking small steps around the front of the mast, stay close to the mast foot with your back to the wind.

Turning Around on the Spot *(Figs 23 (a)–(d))*

The importance of learning to turn around at this stage is obvious – if you don't you might not be able to get back.

1.   Start from the secure position that you were in at the end of the last exercise. Continue holding the mast with both hands and lean it towards the back of the board. As you do this the front of the board will gently turn towards the wind.

2.   As the board begins to turn, take

KEY POINT

Keep your feet close to the mast foot throughout the turn.

---

small steps around the front of the mast, keeping your back to the wind all the time. Take care to keep your feet close to the mast foot.

3.   As the nose of the board passes through the eye of the wind, lean the mast towards the front of the board to make the board turn away from the wind and complete the 180-degree turn.

4.   Once the board is at 90 degrees to the wind again you have completed the

Fig 23 (c)   Lean the mast towards the front of the board and the nose will turn away from the wind.

Fig 23 (d)   The turn has been completed and the board is now facing in the opposite direction.

turn and should now be back in the secure position, but with the board pointing in the opposite direction.

Practise this in both directions so that you are confident that you will be able to turn around and get home again.

Now it's time to get moving!

Practice Exercise

This exercise practises both pulling the sail out of the water and turning on the spot. Start in the kneeling position on the board and pull the sail out. When you feel stable in the secure position, rotate the board through 180-degrees. Drop the sail and repeat the practice in the reverse direction until you feel confident.

KEY POINT

Keep your arms slightly bent, and hold the end of the sail as close to the water as possible. Your weight should be over the middle of the board, and your toes pointing parallel to the boom. Take small steps.

Figs 24 (a)–(e)   Moving off.

Fig 24 (a)   Take your back hand from the mast and use it to balance yourself whilst moving your back foot to a position over the centreboard case.

Fig 24 (b)   Move your front foot until it is just behind the mast foot and is pointing forwards over the centre-line of the board.

Moving Off *(Figs 24 (a)–(e))*

1.   Start again in the secure position. You are now going to sail across the wind in the direction in which your board is pointing. Look along your board and select a goal to head for which is not too far away.

Take your back hand from the mast and use it to help balance yourself. Move your back foot further back over the centreboard case, keeping it over the centre-line.

2.   Move your front foot to just behind the mast keeping your foot pointing forwards on the centre-line of the board.

3.   Turn so that you are facing towards your goal and pull the mast across the board towards the wind until the rig begins to feel light – this is called the 'balance point'.

4.   Put your back hand on the boom and pull it towards you very gently until you can feel the force of the wind in it. Now you are off!

5.   As you start moving, take your front hand from the mast and put it on to the boom. At the same time try and transfer your weight on to your back foot and lean back slightly.

6.   As you approach your goal slow down and stop. Ease out with your back hand and place it on the mast. Put your front hand on the mast and return to the secure position – feet either side of the mast foot, pointing across the board which is at 90 degrees to the wind. Sailing across the wind like this is called sailing on a 'beam reach'.

KEY POINT

As you feel the sail starting to pull you along, put more weight on your back foot and lean back slightly to counteract this force.

Fig 24 (c)   Face your goal and pull the mast across the board into the wind.

Fig 24 (d)   Put your back hand on the boom and pull it towards you in order to start moving.

Fig 24 (e)   Move your front hand from the mast on to the boom. Weight your back foot and lean back slightly.

Steering *(Figs 25 (a) and (b))*

This is a very important skill to have learnt when it comes to avoiding hazards.

As in the turning around exercise, the board is turned by leaning the mast either forwards or backwards. The basic rule to remember is that you lean the mast forwards to turn the board away from the wind and backwards to turn the board into the wind. To make the turn more fluid, use your body-weight.

1. To turn the board into the wind, lean the rig towards the back of the board by extending both arms towards the back and putting weight on your back foot. You may have to lean forwards slightly to keep the board balanced.
2. To turn the board away from the wind, lean the mast towards the front of the board and put more weight on your front foot. Make sure that the sail is correctly sheeted by pulling it in just enough to stop it flapping.

The Theory of Steering

When I was learning to windsurf, I often got confused as to which way I had to move the mast in order to make the board turn. I would have found it a lot easier at the time if I had understood some of the theory of steering – so here is a simple explanation with some diagrams as to why moving the mast back and forth makes the board turn.

Firstly I have to explain that the centre of effort of the sail is an imaginary point where the wind pressure is greatest in the sail. The centre of lateral resistance on the board is an imaginary point where the sideways resistance of the board is greatest. The lateral resistance is largely controlled by the centreboard. When we steer by moving the rig forwards or backwards we move the centre of effort from one side of the centreboard to the other which is the pivot about which the board turns.

In Fig 26 you can see that the centre of effort is directly above the centre of lateral resistance and the board is sailing in a straight line.

Fig 25 (a)   Lean the mast towards the back of the board and weight your back foot to steer the board into the wind.

Fig 25 (b)   Lean the mast towards the front of the board and weight your front foot to steer the board away from the wind.

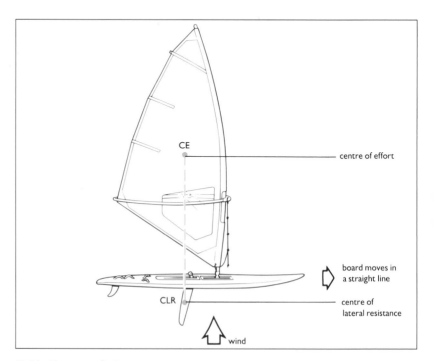

Fig 26   The centre of effort is directly above the centre of lateral resistance, so the board sails in a straight line.

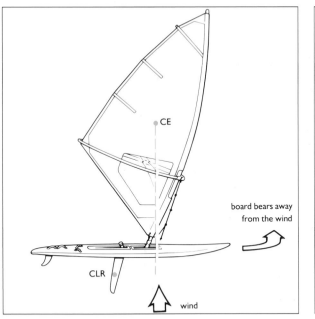

Fig 27   *The centre of effort is in front of the centre of lateral resistance, so the board turns away from the wind.*

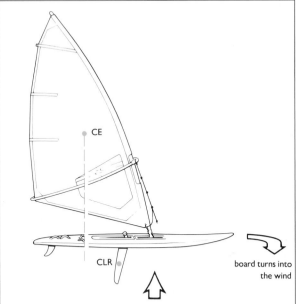

Fig 28   *The centre of effort is behind the centre of lateral resistance, so the board turns into the wind.*

In Fig 27 the sail is leaning forwards and the centre of effort is in front of the centre of lateral resistance. The board is no longer sailing in a straight line and is beginning to turn away from the wind.

In Fig 28 the sail is tilted back and the centre of effort has moved behind the centre of lateral resistance. This has the effect of making the board turn into the wind.

Practise steering by repeatedly sailing an S-shaped course, first turning towards the wind and then away from it by leaning the mast first back and then forwards.

Sailing Upwind

You have already learnt how to sail back and forth across the wind. In case you get blown downwind it is important also to know how to sail upwind.

Fig 29 shows all the directions in which it is possible to sail. As you can see there is an area 45 degrees either side of the wind direction in which it is not possible to sail. If you try to sail at this angle to the wind the sail will stall and you will find yourself

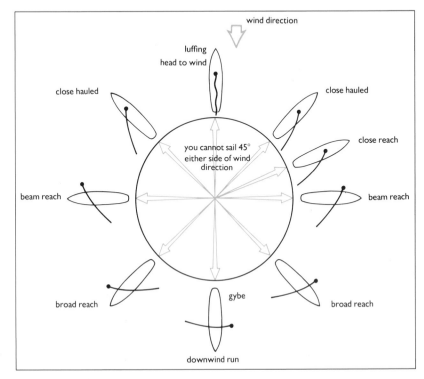

Fig 29   *The directions in which you can sail.*

Sailing backwards. This area is called the 'no-go zone'. To sail upwind you need to sail as close to the wind as possible, in other words on the edge of the no-go zone. This is called a 'close-hauled course'.

Sailing a Close-Hauled Course *(Figs 30 (a) and (b))*

Start from the secure position and sail on a beam reach directly across the wind.

1. For a close-hauled course you need to have the board pointing closer to the wind, so lean the mast towards the back of the board until it has turned so it is around

---

KEY POINT

The further the mast is leaned the further the board will turn, and the quicker the mast is leaned the faster the board will turn.

---

45 degrees off the wind direction.
2. Return the rig to the normal sailing position and pull in slightly with your back hand to keep power in the sail. As you progress you will find that you can feel your way along the edge of the no-go zone by trying to point the board closer to the wind direction by leaning the rig back – when the board slows down you know

it is pointing as high as possible, so you have to lean the mast forwards a little to regain speed.

Tacking *(Figs 32 (a)–(c))*

To make progress directly upwind you need to sail a zig-zag course as you cannot sail in the no-go zone. For example, if you end up directly downwind of the beach from which you started, you will have to sail the course shown in Fig 31 to get back. Changing from course to course like this is called 'tacking'. Tacking is basically the same as turning around on the spot, but it is done from one close-hauled course to the other, rather than from a reach to a reach as you practised before. Tacking is a

Fig 30 (a) Lean the mast towards the back of the board until it is approximately 45 degrees to the wind on a close-hauled course.

Fig 30 (b) If the board turns too far into the wind, lean the mast forwards to turn away.

much faster movement. It is important to tack quickly so that you don't lose ground and end up further downwind!

1.   Start on a close-hauled course and transfer your front hand from the boom to the mast just below the boom. Move your front foot to just in front of the mast so that it is pointing across the centre-line. Lean the rig towards the back of the board.

2.   As the board turns into the wind, put your back hand on the mast and your back foot in front of the mast. Your back should now be facing the wind with your feet pointing towards the back of the board.

3.   Lean the rig towards the front of the board so that the board turns away from the wind. When it is at right angles to the wind you are once again in the secure position, ready to move off on another close-hauled course.

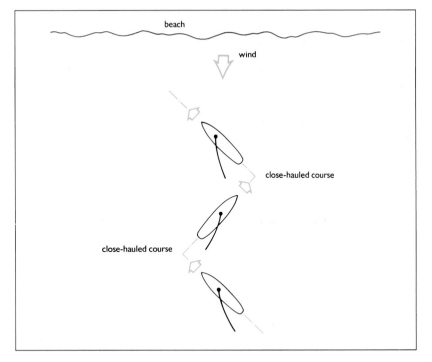

Fig 31   The course you need to sail in order to go directly upwind.

Figs 32 (a)–(c)   Tacking.

Fig 32 (a)   Move your front hand on to the mast and your front foot just in front of it. Lean the rig back.

Fig 32 (b)   Put both hands on the mast and both feet in front of it so that they are pointing towards the back of the board and your back is facing the wind.

Fig 32 (c)   Lean the rig towards the front of the board and return to the secure position.

Fig 33 (a)   Lean the mast towards the back of the board, put your front hand on the mast and your front foot in front of it.

Fig 33 (b)   Keep the sail leaning back and push the tail of the board away from you with your back foot.

Fig 33 (c)   Put your old back hand on the mast and old front hand on the boom.

A Quicker Tack *(Figs 33 (a)–(c))*
Once you are proficient at the normal tack, it is very useful to know a quicker way of tacking so that you can make better progress upwind.

1.   Start from a close-hauled course. Lean the rig towards the back of the board and as you do this put your front hand on the mast and your front foot in front of the mast.
2.   As the board turns, keep the sail leaning down and push the tail of the board away from you with your back foot.
3.   As the back starts to turn away step quickly around the mast and put your old back hand on the mast and front hand on the boom. Take up your new close-hauled course.

KEY POINT

The only way to improve your tacking is through practice. As soon as you get out on the water, warm up with 20 quick tacks.

Sailing Downwind
(Figs 34 (a) and (b))

If you refer to Fig 29 showing points of sailing on page 39 you will see that you have now learnt all the points apart from sailing straight downwind which is sometimes called 'the run'.

1.   Sail on a beam reach and lean the mast forwards to make the board turn away from the wind so that you are on a broad reach.
2.   Ease the sail with your back hand and pull in slightly with your front hand.
3.   Move your feet now so that they are either side of the centreboard case and pointing forwards.
4.   Position the rig so that the sail is at right angles to the board – you are now sailing directly downwind.

Steering Downwind
1.   If you want to turn to the left, lean the rig to the right and put all your weight on your right foot.

2.   If you want to turn to the right, lean the rig to the left and put all of your weight on your left foot.

Gybing *(Figs 35 (a) and (b))*

When you are sailing downwind and want to turn around, it is time-consuming to have to tack. Instead, it is much faster to turn around with the wind behind you so that the stern of the board goes through the eye of the wind – this is called gybing.

1.   Start on a run. When you want to turn put your back hand on to the mast just below the boom.
2.   Guide the mast so that the end of the boom passes over the front of the board. As the board begins to turn, take your front hand from the boom and use it to help balance yourself.
    Shuffle your feet around so that they are back in the secure position.
3.   From the secure position sail away on your new reach.

Fig 34 (a)   Your feet should now be on either side of the centreboard case and pointing forwards.

Fig 34 (b)   Sailing directly downwind with the sail at right angles to the board and the wind behind you.

Fig 35 (a)   Take your back hand from the boom and put it on the mast.

Fig 35 (b)   Take your front hand from the boom and use it to balance yourself as the boom passes over the front of the board.

Figs 36 (a) and (b)   Returning to the beach.

Fig 36 (a)   Retract the centreboard and drop the rig into the water on the leeward side.

Fig 36 (b)   Carry the board out of the water first and then carry the rig out.

Returning to the Beach *(Figs 36 (a) and (b))*

Just as with launching, it is important to do things in the right order when you return to the shore so that you don't damage yourself or your equipment. Don't approach the shore at top speed to impress the crowd.

1.   When the water is about thigh deep,
slow down and return to the secure position. Drop the rig into the water on the leeward side of the board. Make sure the centreboard is retracted.

2.   Dismount and release the mast foot. Carry the board on to the beach and then the rig.

3.   When returning to the car park, carry the rig first and then secure it to something so that it doesn't blow away. Finally go back for the board.

A Bit of Theory

How does the sail power us along? It is easy to understand how the wind can power us along when it comes from directly behind us. However, it is more difficult to understand why we can sail across the wind and even into the wind. The theory is actually surprisingly easy to understand.

The sail is a curved surface in a moving

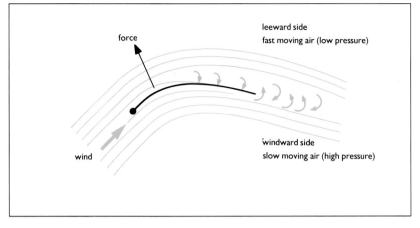

force

leeward side
fast moving air (low pressure)

windward side
slow moving air (high pressure)

wind

KEY POINT

- Lean the mast forwards to bear away and towards the back of the board to head into the wind.

- You cannot sail directly into the wind. The closest to the wind you can sail is 45 degrees either side of it.

- To steer when you are sailing directly downwind, lean the rig and put your weight on the foot which is on the opposite side to that in which you want to turn.

Fig 37   How the sail works.

airflow. It 'bends' the wind which results in a pressure difference between the two sides of the sail. Air always tries to move from high to low pressure which results in a driving force acting at right angles to the sail (*see* Fig 37).

If the sail was put on to a board without a centreboard, the board would travel sideways due to the force in the sail. If the centreboard is put down into a vertical position, the lateral resistance of the board is increased and the board will now travel forwards rather than sideways (*see* Fig 38).

It is important to keep the sail sheeted in at the correct angle so that the air flow is not disturbed and flows smoothly over both sides of the sail.

KIT CHECK

Always wash your wetsuit out with fresh water after use and hang it up to dry inside-out so that the colours do not fade.

Fig 38   The sideways component of the wind (aerodynamic) force is equal to the lateral resistance of the centreboard. The forward component of aerodynamic force is greater than the drag of the hull and this causes the board to accelerate forwards.

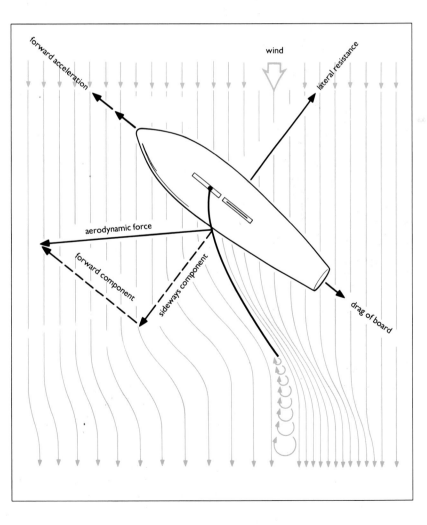

forward acceleration

wind

lateral resistance

aerodynamic force

forward component

sideways component

drag of board

CHAPTER 8

INTERMEDIATE TECHNIQUES

Once you have mastered the basics on the beginner's board you will want to start sailing in stronger winds. This section concentrates on strong wind techniques. You can learn these on your beginner's board but they are easier to master on a lower volume, intermediate's board (*see* Chapter 1). If you are using a beginner's board, remember to attach the footstraps – these make excellent carrying handles as well as helping you stay on the board.

Launching the Rig and Board *(Figs 39 (a) and (b))*

When you are sailing in stronger winds and waves it is easier to launch your board and rig together rather than in two separate units as these will tend to float away from each other.

1. Lay the board deck up across the wind pointing in the direction in which you

are going to launch. Arrange the rig so that the mast lies along the back of the board. Stand on the windward side of the board and take hold of a front footstrap with your front hand and the top of the boom with your back hand.

2. Bend your knees and lift, keeping your back straight. Once you are using your mast track you will find that this is easiest with the mast foot in the front position.

Fig 39 (a)   Take hold of the front footstrap and the top of the boom.

Fig 39 (b)   Bend your knees and lift, keeping your back straight.

Figs 40 (a)–(c)   Launching a heavier board and rig.

Fig 40 (a)   Lay the board on the beach with the rig just off the back of the board.

Fig 40 (b)   Stand between the board and rig, grasp a front footstrap with your front hand and the top of the boom with your back hand.

Launching a Heavier Board and Rig *(Figs 40 (a)–(c))*

There are many different methods of carrying the board and rig but one which is slightly easier with a heavier board is outlined below:

1.   Lay the board on the beach as before with the rig pointing in the same direction, but just off the back of the board.
2.   Stand in the gap between the board and the rig facing the front of the board. Grasp a front footstrap nearest you (on the leeward side) with your front hand, and the top of the boom close to the mast with your back hand.
3.   Bend your knees and lift, remembering to keep your back straight.

KIT CHECK

To work out the amount of volume that you need in an intermediate's board add:

● The weight of the board (kg).
● Your weight plus the weight of your wetsuit and harness (kg).
● The weight of the rig (approximately 9kg).
● The reserve buoyancy for an intermediate's board (this is 40 litres).

The total is the minimum amount of volume that you need.

Fig 40 (c)   Bend your knees and lift with a straight back.

Figs 41 (a)–(e)   The beach start.

Fig 41 (a)   Stand to windward of the board and control it by pushing and pulling on the mast.

Fig 41 (b)   Position the board on a reach, stand close to the board and put your back hand on the boom.

The Beach Start *(Figs 41 (a)–(e))*

There is a much easier way of starting from the beach than uphauling. It is possible to get straight on to the board from the shallows – this is the 'beach start'.

1.   Start with the board and rig in knee-deep water. Make sure that the centreboard is retracted. Stand to windward of the board and rig and manoeuvre it by holding on to the mast above the boom with your front hand. By pushing down on the mast you can make the front of the board turn away from you; by pulling on the mast you can make the board turn towards you.
2.   Position the board so that it is on a reach and walk towards the back of it. Now put your back hand on the boom.
3.   Transfer your front hand on to the boom, lift your back foot on to the board and place it on the centre-line of the

> **KEY POINT**
>
> It is always easiest to walk towards the board than to try to pull it back to you.

board between the front and back straps. At the same time, keep pressure on the mast foot to stop the board from heading into the wind.
4.   Raise the rig by straightening your arms – this will put more power in the sail.
5.   By pushing down on your back foot and front hand, bring your centre of gravity over the board. Lift your front foot

> **KEY POINT**
>
> A common mistake is to put all your weight too far back – this will cause the board to luff up into wind.

on to the board and put it just behind the mast track and lean forwards as you move off.

Let the wind do the work; don't try and pull down on the booms to get on to the board or else you will end up flat on your back!

Steering the Board for the Beach Start

As mentioned previously, you steer the board by either pushing or pulling through the mast foot. Practise turning the board around in shallow water so that you become confident with it. Remember, you should push down on the mast to get the board to turn away from you, and pull towards you to bring the front of the board to you.

Once you have gained control of the board in the water, practise turning it around in complete circles – still in knee-deep water.

Fig 41 (c)   Put your front hand on to
the boom and your back foot on to
the board.

Fig 41 (d)   Straighten your arms to
raise the rig and make it more
powerful.

Fig 41 (e)   Put your front foot on to
the board and lean forwards as you
move off.

Using the Retractable Centreboard

As soon as the wind increases above force
3 it is very hard to sail downwind with the
centreboard in its vertical position, so you
have to learn how to retract it:

1.   Depower the sail and use your back
foot to adjust the centreboard.
2.   Push the centreboard head forwards
to retract it.
3.   Push down and back on the head to
put the centreboard into a vertical
position.

When you are sailing upwind you need
the centreboard fully down in its vertical
position (Fig 42).
   When you are sailing across the wind
on a reach in winds under force 3, you
will need the centreboard half-down. You
also need the centreboard half-down if

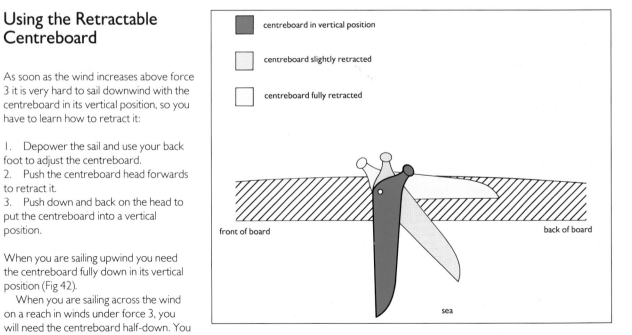

Fig 42   The different centreboard positions.

you are sailing directly downwind in winds under force 3.

When the wind is force 3 or above, you need to have the centreboard fully retracted all the time apart from when you are sailing upwind. On the reaches and when sailing downwind this is the position in which your centreboard should be.

Practice Exercise

Try moving the centreboard with your foot without looking down at it. Concentrate on looking ahead, retract the centreboard and sail for 10 seconds. Still looking ahead, push the centreboard back down into its vertical position, sail for another 10 seconds and then repeat the exercise. Repeat this exercise 10 times without looking down at the centreboard or falling off!

Foot Steering
(Figs 43 and 44)

When you are reaching in stronger winds with the wind coming across you or from behind you and with the centreboard retracted, you can steer the board by weighting your feet instead of leaning the rig. You can either turn into the wind or away from it.

To turn into the wind push down on the windward side of the board with your heels (Fig 43).

To turn away from the wind push down on your toes and bend your knees so that more weight is transmitted to the leeward side of the board (Fig 44).

Practice Exercise

To practise foot steering, turn up into the wind and then away from it so that you are sailing S shapes. You will get used to the feel of the movement and gradually will be able to make larger turns. The more you weight the rail, the more you will turn, but be careful that you don't overdo it or you will get wet!

Fig 43   To foot steer the board towards the wind, push down on the windward edge of the board with your heels.

Fig 44   To steer away from the wind, push down on your toes and bend your knees.

Fig 45   Penny Way racing on the Olympic Lechner board.

Figs 46 (a)–(f)   The flare gybe.

Fig 46 (a)   Throw the rig to windward, sheet in and weight your front foot.

Fig 46 (b)   Move to the back of the board and continue depressing the windward rail.

Fig 46 (c)   Push down on the windward rail and move your hands further down the boom.

Flare Gybing *(Figs 46 (a)–(f))*

This is a much faster way of gybing than the beginner's gybe. It is an ideal way of turning the board quickly in a force 2–3 wind. You may well fall in a few times whilst trying to master this one but it will be worth it in the end!

1.   Start on a close-hauled course and bear away by throwing the rig to windward. Sheet in and keep all your weight on your front foot on the windward rail.
2.   Stay sheeted in and move right to the back of the board. Make sure that you are maintaining foot pressure on the windward rail.
3.   Push down hard on the windward rail and move your hands further down the boom so that you can scoop the rig to windward.

4.   The board will now pivot very quickly around the centreboard and you will find yourself sailing in this clew-first position. Sheet out slightly and move forwards on the board.
5.   Let the rig flip by transferring your back hand from the boom to the mast just below the boom attachment.
6.   As the rig flips, pull the rig across your body and sheet in with your new back hand.

KEY POINT

Do not approach the gybe too quickly or you will rail over – slow yourself down as you enter the turn. If you find that the board turns too quickly, retract the centreboard a little.

Practice Exercise

A good way to practise the flare gybe is by trying to sink the tail of the board. This trick gets you used to standing right on the back of the board. To do a tail sink, sail on a run and with the wind coming from directly behind you, walk as far as you can to the back of the board, still holding the rig. You will find that you can still steer the board from this position.

Sailing in Circles

A good exercise to improve your tacking and gybing is to try sailing in circles.

Practice Exercise

Start with a tack and then do a flare gybe, a tack and then a gybe. Try to do this 3 times in succession without falling off or getting dizzy!

Fig 46 (d)   As the board pivots
quickly, sail in the clew-first position,
sheet out and move forwards.

Fig 46 (e)   Flip the rig by moving your
back hand from the boom to the mast.

Fig 46 (f)   Once the rig has flipped,
pull it across and sheet in.

Harnesses

A harness is the answer to those aching
arms and shoulders – with a harness you
can sail in all winds for hours instead of
having to keep coming in to rest your tired
muscles. Once you have learned the basics
of windsurfing, a harness is easy to use.

What is a Harness?

It is normally made out of foam and nylon
with a hook, and it fits around the chest,
waist or seat. The hook attaches to a loop
of rope that hangs from either side of the
boom – this takes the strain when you are
sailing, leaving your arms to help balance
and steer.

Different Types of Harness

There are three types of harness – the
chest, waist and seat harness. The chest
harness is used by beginners because it is
easy to hook into, and by wave sailors for
the same reason and because it doesn't
restrict movement. The waist harness is
also favoured by wave sailors because it is
very light and unrestricting. The seat
harness is used for racing because it is a
better load carrier. You can sit down in
this harness and use all your body-weight
to counteract the force in the rig (see
Fig 47).

KIT CHECK

Wearing a harness makes windsurfing
much easier. Choose a harness that fits
well and which will not move around or
ride up when you are hooked in.

Fig 47   On the left is a chest harness
and on the right a seat harness.

Harness Lines

You need two harness lines for each rig, one for each side of the boom. They are normally approximately 90cm (35in) long and attach to the boom with velcro holders. They should be made of a thick and durable rope or covered with a plastic tubing to prevent rapid wear. If your harness lines are frayed, replace them immediately – don't wait for them to break at sea!

KIT CHECK

Make sure that your harness lines are of the right length. They should be just long enough so that when you are hooked into your harness your arms are almost straight.

Attaching the lines to the boom

It is very important that the harness lines are positioned correctly on the booms. It is not possible to give an exact distance for them because boom lengths differ with sail sizes. You need the lines to be at the balance point of the rig. If the harness lines are not in the correct position you will find that one arm is taking a lot more strain than the other.

1.   Stand your rig up in a sheltered spot with the mast foot resting against your foot. Hold it as if you were on a reach with your hands shoulder-width apart.
2.   Now slide your hands closer together until you find the point where the rig is balanced (*see* Fig 48).
3.   Mark the balance point with a piece of tape or a marker pen. Lay the rig down and attach the lines either side of this mark, shoulder-width apart.
4.   Check the length of the lines by hooking into them, you should be able to stand comfortably with your arms slightly bent.
5.   Attach lines of the same length to the other side of the boom in the same position.

Fig 48   Slide your hands together along the boom until you find the point where the rig is most balanced.

Figs 49 (a)–(c) Hooking in and unhooking.

Fig 49 (a) Hook into the line by pulling the boom towards you.

Fig 49 (b) Lean back and let the harness take the weight.

Fig 49 (c) Unhook by pulling the boom towards you again.

Hooking In and Unhooking *(Figs 49 (a)–(c))*

When learning to use the harness, one of the greatest fears is of getting stuck in the harness lines. This is very unlikely and almost impossible to do. To increase your confidence in the harness, practise first with it on land.

KEY POINT

Check the position of your harness lines when you are sailing. If you find excess pressure on your front arm, move the harness line nearer the mast. If your back hand is feeling the strain then move the lines further back.

---

1. Hold the rig up in the sand in a reaching position and put your foot up against the mast foot. Place your hands just outside the harness line.
2. Pull the boom towards you to flick the line towards the hook. At the same time move your hips forward so that the harness hook goes over the line and traps it. Do not move your whole body towards the line or you will fall in!
3. Lean back and let the harness take the weight.

Now try to unhook yourself – this is a lot easier than hooking in.

4. Pull the boom towards you again and the line will drop out of the hook.

Practise this until you can do it successfully 5 times in succession, and then try it without looking.

When to Use the Harness

Use the harness when sailing upwind and on a close reach. Do not try and use it on a broad reach or when sailing downwind. You must also remember always to unhook yourself before tacking or gybing.

When practising with the harness do not sail in gusty winds. It is very easy to get catapulted when the wind is gusty and unpredictable.

Mast Tracks

Most modern boards are now fitted with sliding mast tracks. When you are a beginner it is best just to leave the mast foot in the middle position. There is normally a locking mechanism to stop you from accidentally moving the mast foot along the track.

Fig 50 A slalom competitor finds himself airborne in the extreme conditions.

Fig 51   Move the mast foot forwards by pushing down and forwards on the boom.

Fig 52   Move the mast foot back by pulling up and back towards you on the boom.

Why do you Need to Move the Mast Foot?

Moving the mast foot forwards and back in the track allows you to change the waterline length of the board. A longer waterline length improves the upwind performance of the board and a shorter waterline length improves its reaching performance. Therefore you should sail with the mast foot forwards upwind and back on the reaches. The board is also easier to sail when the mast foot is in these positions.

To adjust the mast foot positions (Figs 51 and 52)

Most mast tracks are operated by a pedal at the back of the track. When you press the pedal the mast foot can move and when you release it the mast foot is locked in position.

To move the mast foot forwards, sail on a close reach, put your front foot on the pedal and push down and forwards on the boom. Release the pedal to lock the mast foot (see Fig 51).

To move the mast foot back, sail on a close reach, put your front foot on the pedal and pull up towards you on the boom. Release the pedal again in order to lock the track in the position you want (see Fig 52).

KEY POINT

If the track is stiff you may need to put your knee against the mast to push it forwards. When pulling it back, take one hand off the boom and put it on the mast.

KEY POINT

If the tail of the board is sinking and you are moving too slowly, the mast foot is too far back in the board.

Footstraps

Footstraps are the loops of neoprene that are attached to most boards these days. Apart from making excellent carrying handles they also keep your feet on the board in strong winds and waves. Only attempt to use the footstraps in strong winds (planing conditions) as if you try to use them in lighter winds you will be standing too far back on the board and it will sink at the tail.

Fig 53 shows the footstrap positions usually found on an intermediate's board. The front straps are used only for sailing upwind and the rear straps for reaching. You will notice that there is often a choice of reaching straps. You will find it easier to get into the further forwards straps when you are starting off or in light winds. However, the back straps are the ones to use in strong winds (unless you are very heavy, in which case you will find that the tail will sink when you try and get into them).

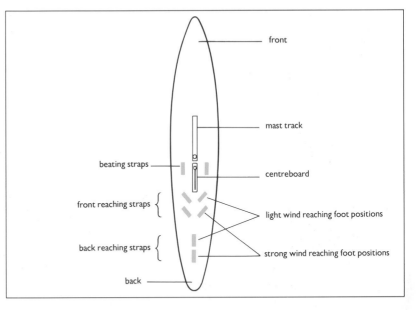

Fig 53   The footstrap positions as they are normally found on an intermediate's board.

KIT CHECK

It is very important to make sure that the footstraps are of the right size. It should only be your toes that protrude through to the other side of the strap. If the straps are too loose you can get your foot trapped on the board and if they are too tight they can be uncomfortable and will prevent you from weighting the board properly.

Adjusting the Straps to the Right Size

Before you try to use the straps it is important to make sure that they are the right size. It should only be your toes that protrude through to the other side of the strap. It can be very dangerous if the straps are too loose as the whole of your foot could slide through and become trapped. If the straps are too tight they are uncomfortable and force you to put too much weight on the windward rail. You have to get them just right.

All footstraps should be adjustable. Put your board skeg down on a piece of grass and lightly put your foot into the strap. Decide by how much you need to adjust the straps and remove your foot. Undo the neoprene covers and you should find velcro or webbing beneath that you can easily adjust.

Getting into the Beating Straps

You should only use these straps when you are sailing upwind – they prevent your feet from getting knocked off the board by a wave or being lifted off the board by the power of the sail.

1.   Sail on a close-hauled course. Make sure the mast foot is forwards, the centreboard vertical and hook in.
2.   Slide your front foot and then the back one into their straps. You will find that these straps enable you to sail in much stronger winds (Fig 54).

Fig 54   Put your front foot into its footstrap first and then put in the back foot.

Fig 55 (a)   Put your front foot into the reaching strap first.

Fig 55 (b)   Keep your weight forwards and slide your back foot into its strap.

Getting into the Reaching Straps
(Figs 55(a) and (b))

Put your mast foot into the back position. Retract your centreboard and sail on a fast reach. If your board has two sets of reaching straps try to get into the front set first. The board in the photographs has only one set of reaching straps.

1.   Put your front foot into the front reaching strap and make sure you are still travelling at speed.
2.   Transfer your weight to your front foot in the strap and gently slide your back foot into the back strap. Keep your weight forwards all the time. When taking your feet out of the straps take your back foot out first and move quickly forwards.

KEY POINT

A common complaint from people starting to use footstraps is that the straps seem to be too far back and the board keeps luffing up into the wind. The answer is to lean further forwards, and to make sure that your centreboard is fully retracted and that your mast track is as far back as possible.

Practice Exercise *(Figs 56 (a) and (b))*

When you are learning how to use your footstraps, the hardest part to get to grips with is the point when you continue to lean forwards and put your weight through the mast foot. If you are not doing this the board will head up into wind. One good exercise to help you practise is this:

1.   Sail on a close reach with your centreboard fully retracted.
2.   Transfer your weight on to your back foot and front hand, and put your front foot into the water on the windward side of the board. To keep the board on a straight course you have to lean forwards and push down with your front hand on to the boom and down through the mast.
3.   Now try to put your foot further into

Fig 56 (a)   Put your front foot into the water on the windward side of the board.

Fig 56 (b)   Put your leg further into the water and apply more pressure through the mast.

the water until your knee and then your thigh disappear. The further your leg goes into the water the more pressure you will have to put through the mast. Try to sail for 200m (200yd) like this and then turn around and try it with the other leg.

Now when you go back and try and use your footstraps you will find it easier to lean forwards and keep the board on a fast course.

Waterstarting

Waterstarting is the method of getting on to the board in deep water without having to use the uphaul. Uphauling in strong winds is both tiring and difficult – waterstarting is a lot easier and more energy-efficient once you have mastered the basics. However, it can only be tried when there is enough wind to pull you out of the water – at least a force 3–5 wind

depending on your weight and sail size. Waterstarting can be practised on any type of board, but is easiest to learn on an intermediate's board where you can resort to the uphaul if you swallow too much water.

Once you have mastered the art of waterstarting the doors are open for you to sail very low volume boards that are exhilarating and much faster, but impossible to uphaul.

Figs 57 (a)–(f)   The rig recovery.

Rig Recovery *(Fig 57 (a)–(f))*

The first part of the waterstart is to get the rig out of the water. Below I explain how to get it out of the water whichever way it falls. Always try to get the rig into position first rather than the board. Once the rig is sorted out you can use its power to position the board.

1.   The worst possible position into which the board and sail can fall is when the board is across the wind and the clew

> **KEY POINT**
>
> If you find it difficult to get the rig out of the water by pulling it over the back of the board, try instead to keep the mast at 90 degrees to the wind and swim upwind whilst holding the mast just above the boom and paddling with your free hand.

facing upwind. The mast needs to be at 90 degrees to the wind before you can

attempt to waterstart. Swim to the boom end and make sure that it is pointing into the wind. Then lift the boom end so that the wind gets underneath it and flips it over.

2.   Holding the mast with one hand and the back of the board with the other, swing the back of the board towards the mast so that they are parallel and across the wind.

3.   To get the rig completely out of the water, hold the back of the board with

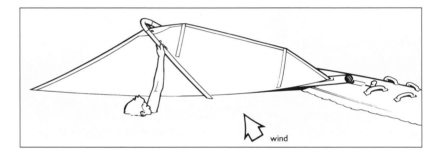

Fig 57 (a)   Lifting the boom end to get the wind underneath it.

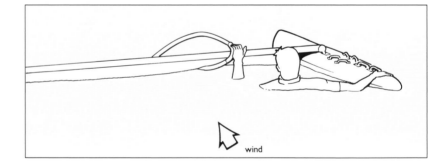

Fig 57 (b)   The rig has now flipped over.

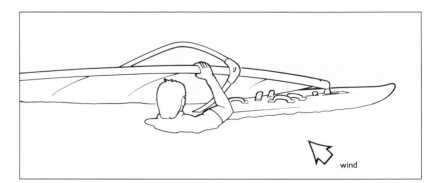

Fig 57 (c)   Getting the rig out of the water.

your back hand and hold the mast with your front hand just above the boom. Pull the rig to windward so that the boom rests over the back of the board – this will allow the wind to get under the rig.

4. Continue to swim the rig to windward until the clew flies clear.

5. Put your back hand on to the boom once the rig is clear of the water.

6. Transfer your front hand from the mast to the boom and push down through the mast foot (as with the beach start) to make the board bear away on to a reach – now you are ready to start.

Practise recovering your rig from the worst possible positions so that you have plenty of confidence in your waterstarting ability. You can practise in shallow water so that you understand where the rig has to be moved in order to get it out of the water.

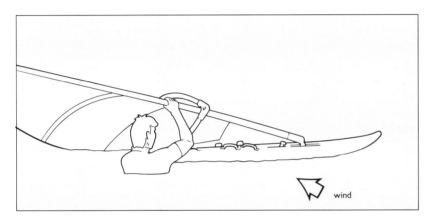

wind

Fig 57 (d)   Swimming the rig to windward.

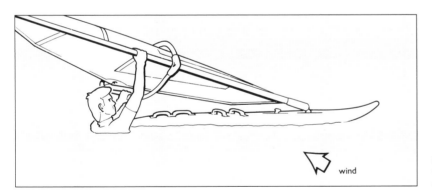

wind

Fig 57 (e)   The rig is now clear of the water and the back hand is on the boom.

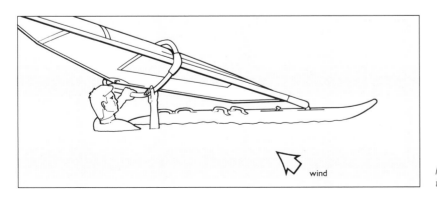

wind

Fig 57 (f)   The front hand is now on the boom and ready to waterstart.

Figs 58 (a)–(d)   The waterstart.

Fig 58 (a)   Steer the rig away from the wind so that the back of the board swings closer to your back foot. Put your back heel on the centre-line between the front and back straps.

The Waterstart *(Figs 58 (a)–(d))*

1.   Keep the mast at right angles to the wind and also keep the whole rig clear of the water to stop the boom end from catching. To stop the board heading into the wind apply pressure through your front arm down the mast. This will help turn the front of the board away from the wind and therefore bring the back of the board closer to your back foot. However, make sure that you don't bear away too much or you will go straight over the front!

2.   Put your back heel over the centre-line of the board between the front and back straps.

3.   Extend your arms to raise the rig higher and give it more power – remember to let the wind do the work!

4.   Crouch over your back leg and kick hard with your front leg.

5.   Lever yourself up and under the boom and put your front foot in front of the straps to get the board moving quickly.

In very strong winds you will find that the wind tends to pick you out of the water instantly and throw you in the water on the other side of the board. To stop this happening, keep the rig low in the water and position your feet in the footstraps before the wind picks you up.

Practice Exercises

Making deeper and deeper beach starts is one way to practise the waterstart without getting too tired. Another way is to sail along and then drop yourself into the water in a kind of reverse waterstart.

Then you practise getting back on to the board. You don't practise rig recovery using this method, but you do get used to getting out of the water.

KEY POINT

- To stop the board heading into the wind you must lean forwards and put lots of pressure through the mast foot.
- When getting the rig out of the water, don't lift the mast too high or the boom end will catch in the water and trip the sail.
- If you are lifted right out of the water by the sail you are probably not keeping the sail low enough in the water – try keeping one foot in the strap.

Fig 58 (b)   Straighten your arms to raise the rig and generate more power.

Fig 58 (c)   Crouch over your back leg and kick hard with your front leg.

Fig 58 (d)   Put your front foot on the board in front of the straps and then you are off!

Fig 59 John Dickens playing in the waves.

The Light Wind Waterstart *(Figs 60 (a)–(c))*

When there is not enough wind to do a proper waterstart you can modify your technique. This is very useful if you are on a low-volume board that you can't uphaul and the wind drops, stopping you from sailing back to shore.

1.   Rig recovery is exactly the same except that you definitely need to rest the rig on the back of the board in order to get it out of the water.
2.   Instead of putting both hands on the boom, put your front hand on the mast below the boom. Slide your front leg and then your back leg on to the board.
3.   As the board starts to move and gain speed it will become more stable so that you can bring yourself into a standing position. Keep your front hand on the mast until you are well under way and then return it to the boom.

KEY POINT

If your board has insufficient volume for uphauling then make sure that you are competent at light wind waterstarts or don't go out on a short board when the wind is marginal.

Stance

Strong wind technique is all about standing properly on the board. If you have a poor stance you will find it hard to complete manoeuvres because the board will keep stalling (*see* Fig 61). Points to concentrate on are:

1.   Always face forwards in the direction that you are going. Look over your front shoulder.
2.   Your shoulders should always be parallel to the sail; their angle depends on the point of sail you are on.

Figs 60 (a)–(c)   The light wind waterstart.

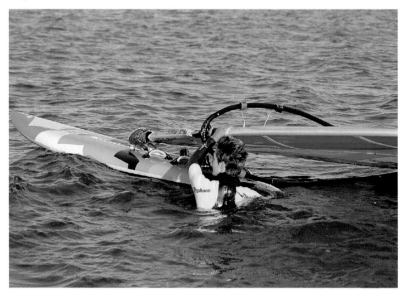

Fig 60 (a)   Rest the rig on the back of the board.

Fig 61   Strong wind stance.

3.   Your arms should always be extended (as mentioned in the section on harnesses earlier in this chapter) so that any strain is taken by the stronger shoulder and back muscles instead of the weaker arm muscles. Try to keep the rig upright all the time for maximum power.
4.   Your back should remain straight all the time. As the wind increases you should sit down more in your harness.
5.   Your hands should always be shoulder-width apart on the boom.
6.   Your legs should always be slightly bent so that they are ready to react to waves or gusts.
7.   Your feet should also be approximately shoulder-width apart. A wider stance may feel more stable but it is not as speed-efficient as having all your weight close together.

In lighter winds it is better to have your weight further forwards; as the wind increases it is faster to move back on the board.

Fig 60 (b)   Hold the sail with your front hand on the mast and back hand on the foot, then slide your legs over the board.

Fig 60 (c)   As you gain speed, bring yourself up into a standing position.

Closing the Gap *(Fig 62)*

This is a phrase often mentioned in windsurfing conversations.

The 'gap' is the space between the bottom of the sail and the board. The theory is that a gap creates a lot of turbulence and when this is closed the windsurfer becomes more efficient. Whatever the theory, it is definitely true that if you can close this gap your speed increases!

1.   You can only try this in planing conditions. Sail on a reach with your centreboard retracted, hooked into your harness and in your footstraps.
2.   Angle the rig back past your body until the boom is almost touching the water and lean forwards.

This is a very fast, reaching stance so it is well worth spending time and effort perfecting it.

Fig 62   Close the gap by pulling the rig down so that the sail is almost touching the water and board.

Figs 63 (a)–(f)   The carve gybe.

Fig 63 (a)   Push down on your toes to transfer your weight so that it is nearer the centre of the board.

Fig 63 (b)   Put your weight on to your back foot on the leeward rail and push your knees forwards.

Fig 63 (c)   Keep your knees driving inwards throughout the turn.

The Carve Gybe *(Figs 63 (a)–(f))*

This is one of the most exhilarating high-wind manoeuvres and is the easiest way to turn your board around in strong winds. The turn is very fluid and resembles turning a ski or skateboard by weighting the inside edge. Earlier in this chapter you learnt how to foot steer your board; you can now use this technique to turn the board through 180 degrees.

To perform a perfect carve gybe takes a lot of practice, so don't get too despondent on the way there. Ideal conditions in which to learn are a force 4–6 wind and flat water. Learn the manoeuvre on an intermediate's board, but as you progress you will find it easier to perfect on a shorter, lower volume board.

1.   Sail on a reach, unhook from your harness and check that there are no obstacles in the path of your turn.
2.   Bear away on to a broader reach by pushing on your toes and bringing your body-weight more over the centre of the board.
3.   Take your back foot out of the rear strap and place it on the leeward rail in line with the back strap – point it slightly forwards. Start the turn by transferring all your weight on to this foot. Push your knees forwards and towards the inside of the turn.
4.   Your upper body should remain upright or should lean slightly forwards throughout the turn, but you should keep your knees driving inwards. Hold the rig upright throughout the turn and sheet out as the board turns on to its new reach.
5.   On the new reach, transfer your back hand from the boom to the mast. This will allow the rig to flip when you begin to

> **STAR TIP**
>
> *The quickest way to learn to perfect the carve gybe is by practising on flat water in a moderate breeze. Before setting to sea, try and mentally picture what you have to do.*
>
> Dave Hackford
> *Boards, 53, 1988.*

Fig 63 (d) Move your back hand from the boom to the mast to let the rig flip.

Fig 63 (e) Move your old front hand on to the new side as the new back hand.

Fig 63 (f) Pull the rig across your body and sheet in, then put your mast hand on to the boom.

move your feet into their new footstrap positions.

6. Release the boom with the old front hand and position it as the new back hand on the other side.

7. Pull the rig forward and across your body to sheet in, and then as you gain speed move your hand from the mast on to the booms as well. Once you are planing, hook in and get back into the straps on the new tack.

As mentioned before, the carve gybe is not learnt overnight. In order to succeed you need commitment. Visualize the move and try it at speed. The worst that can happen is that you get wet! Don't stay too long in the clew-first position as this is very unstable.

Once the board has turned, quickly change your foot positions so that the board does not over-rotate. Look for flat water for the turn – it is a lot easier than turning on chop. If you are falling in on the inside of the turn it is because you are bending your whole body into the turn instead of just your knees.

Practice Exercise

To practise bending your knees properly into the turn, try to touch the water on the inside of the turn with your knees. You will never actually get down this far but the exercise will give you the correct body position.

You must give 100 per cent when practising, and the best way to improve and to make your board turn more smoothly and quickly is to fall off a lot when you practise. This is not the most enjoyable thing to do on a wet and cold day, but it will certainly pay off!

Fig 67   Competitors in line for a start of the Mistral one design class.

find out whether you are allowed to pump or not from the organisers.

Pumping in Wind and Waves

In competitions where pumping is allowed you can gain a lot of ground on the reaches by pumping properly. Pumping is a skill that takes a long time to perfect; when you first try it you may even go slower than you did without pumping. However, once you acquire the skill you will notice the difference.

When you are sailing on a reach and the back of your board is lifted by a wave, this

---

STAR TIP

On the subject of pumping: *Imagine you are trying to gather the wind in a pillow case, using a scooping circular movement.*

Dee Caldwell
Windsurf, 66, 1987.

---

is the time to pump!

Pull the sail sharply towards you – this will instantly create more wind and more power – then let the sail out again. Always remember that you should pump at the

top of a wave to help accelerate your board down the next face. Pumping at the bottom of a wave does not work!

Practice Exercise

Pumping is not an easy skill and it requires a lot of practice if you are to do it well. On a day when the wind has dropped, stay out for a bit longer and practise your pumping technique. Set yourself a target, such as the other side of the lake or a marker buoy. Once you have been practising for a while you will be amazed by your improvement! It is also good aerobic exercise fitness.

CHAPTER 9

ADVANCED TECHNIQUES

Once you have mastered the skills of waterstarting and gybing, it is time to try and sail a lower volume board in stronger winds and waves. These boards are very exhilarating to sail – they are much faster and more manoeuvrable than higher volume boards. Advanced techniques such as duck and slam gybing can be tried on an intermediate's board, but for wave sailing you really do need a lower volume board and wave rig similar to those shown on pages 14 and 17. If you are using a low-volume board, experiment with it first on inland waters until you are confident. You will notice that a higher level of fitness is needed as you will be sailing in stronger winds most of the time.

KIT CHECK

To work out the amount of volume that you need in an advanced wave board add:

- The weight of the board (kg).
- Your weight plus the weight of your wetsuit and harness (kg).
- The weight of the rig (around 9kg).
- The reserve buoyancy that you require (15 litres if you want to be able to uphaul; 3 litres if you just want to be able to float home if the wind drops).

The total figure will be the minimum amount of volume that you need in your board.

Practice Manoeuvres

You will find immediately that the lower volume board is a lot more responsive than boards on which you have previously sailed. Practise your beach starts, waterstarts and gybes on flat water before taking your low volume board out to sea; every board is different to sail so it might take a bit of getting used to. If the wind isn't as strong as you would like, try uphauling – if you are light you may find it very easy, but if you are heavy it may be impossible. It is important to know if it is possible to uphaul so that you are aware of your options if you are out to sea and the wind drops.

Uphauling a Low-Volume Board *(Figs 68 (a) and (b))*

1.   Make sure the board is pointing in the direction in which you want to go, because if the wind is dropping you don't want to waste time sailing in the wrong direction. You will find it hard to balance on the board so be cautious in your movements.
2.   Pull yourself on to the board keeping your weight over the centre-line – try to trim the board so that neither end is too far under the water. Bring yourself to your knees, take hold of the uphaul line and gradually bring yourself to your feet. You will need a wide stance to keep yourself and the board balanced.
3.   Lift the rig out of the water, taking care not to fall in backwards as the boom end jerks clear. Quickly put your hands on to the boom and try to pick up speed as rapidly as possible.

When you practise uphauling your board, do it in shallow water so that you can walk home if you can't do it and there is not enough wind to waterstart!

Fig 68 (a)   When uphauling keep a wide stance in order to spread your weight.

Fig 68 (b)   Once the rig is up, put your hands on the boom and pick up speed.

Figs 69 (a)–(d)   Tacking a short board.

Fig 69 (a)   Move your feet forwards, weight the windward rail and lean the rig back.

Fig 69 (b)   Put your front hand on the mast and your front foot in front of the mast.

Fig 69 (c)   Change your foot positions quickly and throw the rig forwards to bear away.

Fig 69 (d)   Move both feet further down the board and sheet in.

Tacking a Short Board
(Figs 69 (a)–(d))

Another useful manoeuvre to practise on inland waters is the short-board tack. It is very useful if you want to sail upwind as you don't lose the ground to windward when you turn around as you do in a gybe.

The short-board tack is basically a speeded-up version of the long-board tack, except for the obvious difference that you have less volume in a short board so it is less stable. This means that you must spend less time in front of the mast and the tack has to be quicker.

1.   Start the turn from a planing reach. Move both feet forward of their straps, weight the windward rail with your heels and incline the rig back to turn the board.
2.   Grab the mast below the boom with your front hand and put your front foot in front of the mast. As the board goes into the eye of the wind, prepare to bring your back foot up to your front foot.
3.   Remember both feet must never be together in front of the mast for more than a fraction of a second, so as soon as the back foot moves forward, your front foot must move back on to the new side of the board as you pivot around the mast. Take the mast or front of the boom with your front hand and throw it forwards so that the board bears away,
4.   Move both feet further down the board and sheet in.

KEY POINT

Perform a short board tack quickly – if you wait too long on the original tack the board will slow down too much. Approach the turn with speed and try to keep your speed up throughout as this will give you more stability.

Fig 70   An aerial gybe – a difficult short-board manoeuvre.

Fig 71   Peter Hart gybing in the waves.

Fig 74   Speed sailing on the windy Weymouth speed course.

Figs 75 (a)–(f)   The duck gybe.

Fig 75 (a)   Begin to carve the board as for a normal gybe.

Fig 75 (b)   Cross your hands over to grab the back of the boom.

Fig 75 (c)   Release with the old back hand and pull the boom across while stretching through to the new side.

The Duck Gybe *(Figs 75 (a)–(f))*

This is another trick with which to impress the crowds. Once you have mastered the carve gybe, the duck gybe is surprisingly easy. It is easiest to perform on a very short-boomed sail with no long foot battens.

> **KEY POINT**
>
> Carve the board just as for a normal gybe, making sure that you lean into the turn. Keep planing throughout the gybe as speed is very important when flipping the rig. Stay low throughout the turn to avoid having to lean back to duck under the rig – if you lean back you will stall the rig.

1.   Start from a fast reach and carve the board into a turn as you would do for the normal carve gybe. As the board turns, slide your back hand right to the back of the boom.
2.   When the board is pointing downwind and the rig appears weightless (this happens because the board is travelling at the same speed as the wind), cross your front hand over your back hand and grab the clew end of the boom.
3.   Let go with your old back hand and pull the boom across your face and back towards the tail. This allows you to stretch through to the new boom with the rig correctly set up for the new tack.
4.   Grab the new boom with your new front hand and then with your back hand.
5.   Sheet in and continue to carve the board around on to its new course.
6.   Move your feet into their new positions.

Practice Exercise

It is a good idea to familiarize yourself with the hand movements of the duck gybe on land before attempting it on water. Find a sandy or grassy area free of bodies and position your rig so that you have plenty of room.

> **KIT CHECK**
>
> The duck gybe is best performed on a short boomed sail with no long foot battens that could hit you in the face whilst ducking.

Sailing in Waves

Once you are confident about sailing a low-volume short board it is time to go

Fig 75 (d)   Take hold of the new side with your front hand and then your back hand.

Fig 75 (e)   Sheet in and continue to carve the board.

Fig 75 (f)   Move your feet into their new positions.

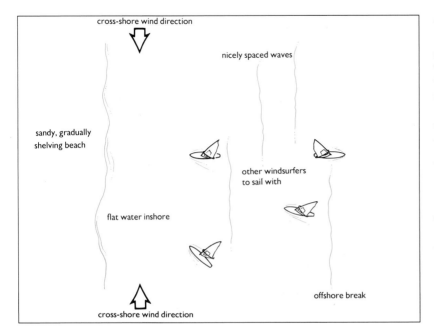

Fig 76   A safe wave venue.

and have some fun in the waves. The waves add a new dimension to windsurfing. It does take a long time to master sailing in waves, but it can be very rewarding so long as you know your limits and don't try and go out in conditions that are far beyond them! Sailing in waves can be dangerous if you try to sail beyond your limits – so be sensible!

Choosing your Launch Spot

When you go out in waves for the first time select an easy place to sail – somewhere where the wind is constant and the waves easy and forgiving. The best way to find out about such a place is to ask at your local windsurfing club. Points to look for are:

1.   A cross-shore wind of force 4 or more – an onshore or offshore wind is of no use.
2.   A sandy, gradually shelving beach.
3.   Waves that are nicely spaced and not dumping.
4.   Other people to sail with.
5.   No strong tides, currents or rips that could carry you out to sea.
6.   Waves no bigger than 1m (3ft) in height.

Ideally an offshore break over a sandbar or ledge is better for gaining confidence as you have flat water from which to launch. The flat water gives you time to get settled and pick up speed before encountering the waves. It also gives you a bit of breathing space and a retreat if you find yourself in trouble.

STAR TIP

There is so much to develop in wave-riding that you can't get bored with it.
Mark Woods
On Board, 7(4), 1986.

Launching in Waves

A point of safety here: never get yourself into a position where you are caught between the rig and the beach with the waves pushing the rig towards you. Avoid this situation at all costs even if it means letting your board and rig wash up on the beach.

If you have no choice but to launch through the waves here is how to do it:

1.   Carry the board and rig into the water as with the beach start but don't let them down into the water until there is a flat spot from which to launch. Waves come in sets, once a few big ones have passed there will be a lull before the next ones. You should launch in this lull (Fig 77).
2.   The key to a successful beach start in waves is to get on quickly during the lull and to get going as fast as possible before the next wave comes.
3.   If you don't make the launch this first

Fig 77   Wait for a flat spot before you launch.

time you will have to wait for the next lull. To stop your board from being washed around by the waves, concentrate on keeping the nose pointing into the waves with both hands on the boom for better control. When a clear patch arrives quickly hop on making sure that the skeg is in plenty of water!
4.   As you power up and sail out through the waves remember to keep the nose of the board heading into them so that they don't knock you off sideways. Keep plenty of power on so that you have enough speed to get through the waves.

KEY POINT

If the wind is slightly onshore, work out on which tack you are going to set off before getting into the water.

Coming Back to Shore

Coming back in through the waves can also cause a few problems although this time you have the power of the waves working with you instead of against you. If

you are on a wave try to slow down so that it overtakes you – you don't want to be on a wave that dumps you on the beach! As soon as you get into knee-deep water, jump off and push or carry the board to safety. Don't delay in the shallows as you will quickly be caught by the following wave. Whatever happens make sure that you keep your rig out of the water as this can easily break in the shorebreak.

KIT CHECK

It is a good idea to wear a crash helmet with a face guard when you are sailing in waves. It will protect you if you fall on top of your equipment or if you are hit by another airborne sailor.

Jumping

Once you have mastered the art of getting in and out of the shorebreak you can begin to have fun in the waves. Jumping is one of the easiest but most impressive skills to learn, provided that you have good conditions. As mentioned earlier, waves on a sandbar or ledge are easier to learn in because the flat water that usually surrounds them can be used both for increasing speed and as an escape route. Don't sail in waves that are too big when you are beginning; you learn more when you are full of confidence than when you are scared silly. Waves of 1m (3ft) in height are plenty big enough.

KEY POINT

● Always be on the look out for waves that will make good ramps.
● If you can't get the board out of the water you either are not going fast enough or you are not tilting the board enough on take off to get the wind underneath it.

Choosing your wave

When you are learning to jump you will probably find that you don't even have to

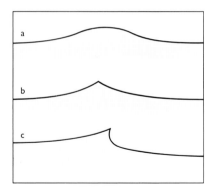

Fig 78 (a) A rolling wave; (b) A small wave with a peak; (c) A steep wave with a peak.

try to become airborne. If you hit the right kind of wave you will find yourself up in the skies wondering what to do next. Waves with peaks provide much better ramps than those without them.

Fig 78(a) shows a rolling wave without a peak. This is a hard wave to jump. Fig 78(b) shows a small wave with a peak, this is an easy wave to jump and is ideal for beginners as it is a small wave. Fig 78(c) shows a steep wave with a good peak. This is an ideal wave for the more advanced wave sailor.

To jump well you need to be travelling at speed. If you are sailing waves on a bar or ledge it is easy to pick up speed on the flatter water in front of them. If you are sailing at a venue where the waves are only close to the shore then it is more difficult to pick up speed before a wave. The answer is to try to select your wave and then bear away before hitting it to increase speed. Try to avoid other smaller waves that might slow down your approach.

How to jump (Figs 79 (a) and (b))

1. Sail on a reach with your feet in the straps. The further apart your feet are the more leverage you have when jumping.
2. Look for your wave and head for it – aim for a section just slightly downwind. If

STAR TIP

Anybody or anything will start to fly if they hit a ramp at speed; control and landing are the arts that make the whole process enjoyable.

Peter Hart
Windsurf, 66, 1987.

you try to head upwind you will lose speed immediately.
3. Carve the board towards the wind and up the face of the wave – this will help the wind to get under the nose of the board.
4. Unhook and bend your knees slightly as you hit the wave. As the nose goes up the wave, pull up and angle your front foot to lift the windward rail. The wind can now get underneath and help lift the board.
5. Pull the rig over the top of your body and sheet in to increase height.

Fig 79 (a) Unhook and bend your knees as you hit the wave.

Fig 79 (b) Pull the rig over your body and sheet in to increase your height.

Figs 80 (a) and (b)   Preparing to come down.

Fig 80 (a)   Level the board out by picking up your heels.

Fig 80 (b)   Lean back, bend your knees and sheet in for a tail-first landing.

Preparing to come down
(Figs 80 (a) and (b))

1.   Allow the nose of the board to be swung around in the air so that you are heading slightly downwind for landing.
2.   Pick your heels up and bend your back leg to level the board up.
3.   The easiest way to land is with the board flat, but the impact of this hard landing can damage your board. The best way to land therefore is nose first, but this is difficult and uncertain when you are just beginning. Tail-first landings are the safest to do at this stage.

RULES CHECK

If you are sailing with other people on the waves it is important that you all take notice of the basic rule that keep clear of boards going out.

---

4.   Lean back and sheet in a little so that the tail hits the water. Depower the sail and bend your knees to use as shock absorbers, this will help prevent spin-out.

KEY POINT

If the board spins out on landing it is likely that you have too much weight on the tail. Bend your legs more on impact and lean forwards immediately.

Fig 81   An upside-down jump. As you reach the peak of a wave, lean back and pull the boom back over your head.

An Upside-Down Jump
(Fig 81)

Once you are at home in the waves, your confidence will build and you will want to try to do some of the tricks that the experts are up to. One of the easiest of tricks is the upside-down jump which just requires that you hit the right wave, lean back and hang on!

1.   Pick a steep wave and hit it with speed. As you reach the peak of the wave lean back and pull the boom back over your head. You will now be upside-down!
2.   To return to Earth, control the board by shifting your weight to the back of it. As the board comes down prepare to land (Fig 81).

Gybing on Waves

Once you have jumped out through the waves you will have to gybe around in order to return to the shore. Once you have become used to waves and the timing of them it is easier to gybe on them than on flat water. This is because the speed of the wave will keep the board planing and stable throughout the turn.

1. Approach the wave on a reach at speed. With 3–4 board lengths to go before the wave, begin your turn.
2. As soon as the nose begins to rise up the face of the wave, release your back hand whilst continuing the carve (Fig 82).
3. As you exit from the gybe you may have to lean back slightly to prevent the board from nosediving.

Riding the Waves

Now that you can successfully gybe on to a wave that will take you back to shore, you can have some fun on it instead of just using it to carry you along. Riding on

Fig 82 Gybing on to the face of a wave.

Fig 83 John Dickens riding the waves at Kimmeridge Bay.

Figs 84 (a) and (b) A bottom turn and cutback.

Fig 84 (a) A bottom turn – carving a turn at the bottom of a wave.

Fig 84 (b) A cut back – carving a turn at the top of a wave.

> **KEY POINT**
>
> When you attempt to wave gybe, you will probably find that the wave overtakes you. To prevent this, start the turn earlier.

waves can be just as much fun if not more fun than jumping them. If after your gybe you find yourself ahead of the wave you wanted to be on, you may have to slow down so that you can ride it.

Once you are on a wave the tail of the board will be picked up and the board will accelerate down the wave's face. As you suddenly accelerate you will have to move back to stop the nose from diving. You will also have to sheet in as the apparent wind will change due to your increase in speed.

To make the best use of the wave, sail along the wave face. If you want to get off the wave either sail down the face of it

and accelerate away or slow down and drop off behind it. If the face is beginning to turn into white water, it is best to avoid it as white water is very difficult to sail in.

A Bottom Turn and Cutback *(Figs 84 (a) and (b))*

As you become more proficient you can try to turn up and then down the face of the wave. The S shape turns that are made are called bottom turns and cut backs. Start with a bottom turn:

1. As you sail down the face of the wave, footsteer the board as if you were going to do a carve gybe so that the board points back up to the top of the wave. Do not flip the rig. As you approach the top of the face turn again so that you are heading back down the face.
2. To turn, switch all your weight to the windward rail. This will turn the board

sharply back down the face of the wave. When you reach the bottom of the wave perform another bottom turn to continue riding the wave.

When you are trying this be careful that you don't end up in the 'rinse cycle' (the powerful white water that can spin you faster than your washing machine!). This is bound to happen at some time; my recommendation is to make sure that you hold on to your mast tip all the time and try to stay on the wave side of your board.

When you hear a big wave coming and you are in the water, dive down with your mast tip to avoid the lip washing you around. Don't let go of your equipment or else you will have a long swim. The big waves normally come in sets of 2–5, so if you can just hang on to your equipment and let them pass you will be able to get back up and going after quite a short time.

CHAPTER 10

INTRODUCTION TO COMPETITION

Once you have mastered the skills of windsurfing in most conditions you may find that the only way to improve further is to enter competitions. Not everybody is competitive but for those who are, there are windsurfing competitions for every ability, age, sex and interest. As well as being an excellent way to improve, competitions give you the opportunity to meet people who share your interest in the sport.

A History of Competition

Windsurfing competitions started soon after the invention of the windsurfer. The windsurfer board was the obvious vehicle for competition, being light, fast and responsive. Competitions started on conventional yacht-racing triangular courses, and as the sport progressed, long-distance races were introduced which took the sailors along miles of coastline.

Freestyle was the next discipline to become popular – this is a kind of gymnastic display on the board which needs flexibility, imagination and a fearless attitude. Each sailor performs a 3-minute routine in turn and is marked by a panel of judges.

Slalom was the fourth discipline sailed on the windsurfer. This takes place around a rather complicated six-buoy course demanding both upwind and downwind turning ability. At the World and European Championships, competitors compete for individual and overall discipline titles.

The windsurfer and windsurfer racing were very popular in America and

Australia, but meanwhile in Europe a form of development racing was becoming popular. Course racing was the only discipline, but the rules allowed any type of design of board to enter. This was (and still is) known as Division II racing.

In 1982 the decision was made to include windsurfing in the 1984 Olympics for the first time; the board chosen for this event was the Windglider. Only one person from each country was allowed to enter. Windsurfing has been in the Olympics ever since, with the Lechner Division II board being chosen for the 1988 and 1992 games.

A professional side to windsurfing competition has developed from these original competitions. The professional competitions are only sailed in high winds so that the action is spectacular. The international circuit of events is known as the World Tour. Competition only takes place in winds of over 11 knots and consists of three disciplines – course racing, slalom and wave sailing. There are individual discipline winners and overall winners.

Besides the Olympic and World Tour events there are also production funboard events. These are sailed on standard production boards with no modifications and the disciplines are course racing and slalom. This kind of racing is very suitable for competitors aspiring to enter world cup competitions.

Speed sailing is another form of windsurfing competition. Sailors are timed along a straight 500m (550yd) course, the winner being the competitor with the fastest time.

Below are explanations of all of the different forms of windsurfing competition.

Freestyle Windsurfing

Freestyle used to be a very popular form of international competition with professional sailors concentrating solely on this discipline. However, since the funboard boom the art of freestyle has almost been forgotten. Freestyle is still great fun to try on windless days, especially as a way to improve your balance and board-handling skills.

There are two types of freestyle competition – either individual, where each person performs in turn, or knockout where all competitors perform together and anyone who cannot perform a requested trick is knocked out.

Individual Freestyle

Each competitor has 3 minutes in which to perform their routine in front of a panel of judges. They are judged on the difficulty of the tricks performed and on their overall impression. It is very important to link all the tricks together in a fluid manner.

Knockout Freestyle

All the competitors sail together in front of the judges. The organiser shouts out a trick and everyone must perform it. Anyone who does not complete the trick or who falls into the water is disqualified.

RULES CHECK

In knockout freestyle competitions a competitor who fails to perform a trick is disqualified.

The organizer continues to announce tricks (which become progressively harder) until only the winner is left.

The tricks performed in freestyle competitions are:

1.   The railride – standing on the edge of the board instead of on the deck. This is not a difficult trick to perform but looks very impressive (Fig 85).
      There are many more difficult variations to this standard trick, they are:

a)   Backwards railride – sailing backwards on the rail.
b)   Clew-first railride – sailing on the rail with the sail in a clew-first position.
c)   Head dip on the rail – sailing on the rail and crouching down to do a head dip.
d)   Splits on the rail – doing the splits whilst sailing on the rail.

2.   Clew first – sailing with the boom pointing towards the front of the board (Fig 86).

3.   Sailing back to front – sailing with your back towards the sail and head facing out (Fig 87).

4.   Lying down on the board – lying down on your board whilst holding the rig with your feet (Fig 88).

5.   Sitting down on the board – sitting on the board whilst holding the rig below the boom by the mast and foot of the sail (Fig 89).

6.   Kneeling on the board – kneeling on the board whilst holding the rig by the boom and the mast (Fig 90).

7.   Head dip – sailing on a reach and leaning over backwards to put your head into the water (Fig 91).

8.   Pirouette – letting go of the rig, then spinning around on the ball of your foot so that you catch the rig again (Fig 92).

Fig 85   A rail ride – standing on the edge of the board.

Fig 86   Clew first – sailing with the back of the sail pointing towards the front of the board.

Fig 87   Sailing back to front – sailing with your back to the sail and facing out.

Fig 88   Lying down on the board holding the boom with your feet.

Fig 89   Sitting on the board holding the rig below the boom.

Fig 90   Kneeling on the board.

Fig 91   A head dip.

Fig 92   A pirouette.

9. Duck tack – tacking the board by passing the rig over your head instead of over the front of the board (Fig 93).

10. Spin tack – performing a pirouette around the front of the mast as the board is tacked (Fig 94).

11. Body drag – this can only be done in winds of over force 4. You remove your feet from the board and allow your body to drag alongside of the board before stepping back on to the board (Fig 95).

12. Somersault through the booms – this is often performed as the final trick because of the extreme likelihood of getting wet! You do a somersault around the booms to land back on the board.

13. Stepping out of the booms – this is also performed as a dismount. Sail inside the booms facing out and then step over the booms to stand on the normal side of the booms. Sometimes this trick is turned into a tail sink.

Another type of freestyle is 'tandem freestyle' when two people get on a board together and perform tricks. This is great fun to try with a friend and can provide some very impressive and entertaining results. Some of the tricks possible are:

1. Standing on the shoulders of your partner and holding on to the top of the mast (Fig 96).

2. Standing on your partner's knees, inside of the boom and facing out.

3. A two-person railride.

4. Each person standing either side of the sail performing a separate trick.

Fig 93   A duck tack – tacking by passing the boom over your head.

Fig 94   A spin tack – spinning in front of the mast whilst tacking the board.

Fig 95   A body drag – letting the power of the sail drag you along through the water.

Fig 96   *Tandem freestyle – standing on the shoulders of your partner.*

RULES CHECK

In long-distance races and marathons all the competitors start together. The first one to the finish line is the winner.

with the weather conditions. Most events of this type cater for a large number of competitors and include a lot of straight-line sailing so there is little need for the skills necessary for rounding marks. The start and finish line is often on the beach which creates excitement for the spectators.

Speed Sailing

Speed sailing has become purely a high wind form of competition. It is all about breaking world records (the current world record on a 500m (550yd) course is 40.33 knots) and so competitors don't take to the water until the conditions are suitable – at least 25 knots of wind and flat

STAR TIP

I've been speed sailing for five years and I've only ever seen three days where the conditions for record breaking were perfect.

Eric Beale
Windsurf, 84, 1989.

water. Because of the necessary conditions, speed events have to be held at suitable venues such as West Kirby where there is an elevated marine lake or Portland Harbour where the water is flat. If the water is choppy, the specialized boards that are necessary for high speeds fly out of the water and are therefore very hard to sail.

Equipment

As mentioned above, speed sailing equipment is very specialized. The boards resemble water skis in their shape, weight

RULES CHECK

You should be aware of the basic rules before you first race. There is a complete rule book available from the International Yacht Racing Union (IYRU) that you should read if you decide to progress with your racing.

Long-Distance Racing or Marathons

Long-distance races or marathons are run over courses of varying formats; most are around specific landmarks such as islands or along stretches of coastline. There is no set length for this type of race and it varies

KIT CHECK

A speed board is approximately 280cm (110in) long and between 30–40cm (12–16in) wide. The sails are camber induced with up to ten full length battens.

and size. A normal speed board is approximately 280cm (110in) long and 30–40cm (12–16in) wide. The rigs that go with the boards are specifically designed for high-speed reaching. The sails are camber induced with up to ten full-length battens to maintain a constant flow shape. A sail suitable for breaking the world record would have an area of only 3.5–4.6 sq m (37.7–49.5 sq ft) because of the high winds necessary for record breaking.

The Course

Because competitors need to sail in very flat water, the course is as close to the shore as possible. The actual course is either 250m (270yd) or 500m (550yd) long but world records can only be recognized if they are set on the 500m (550yd) course.

The competitors reach from one end to the other as quickly as possible and are timed for each run. The competitor with the fastest time when the course closes is the winner.

RULES CHECK

A world speed record can only be ratified on a 500m (550yd) course. The competitors sail as fast as they can from one end to the other and are timed on each run.

Olympic Competition

Windsurfing has been an Olympic sport since 1984. Racing is held whatever the conditions as the board and rig used are suitable for all wind strengths.

The board used in the 1988 and 1992 Olympics is called the 'Lechner A390'. It is a large course racing board with 350 litres of volume so it even sails well in very light winds. The rig used is a 7.3 sq m (78.6 sq ft) lightweight camber-induced sail.

The original Olympic course used to be the standard yacht racing triangle (Fig 97). This has since been modified to the course

KIT CHECK

The board used in the 1988 and 1992 Olympics is called the Lechner. It is a large course racing board with a volume of 350 litre. The sail measures 7.3 sq m (78.6 sq ft).

Fig 97   The Olympic triangle course.

shown in Fig 98 which puts more emphasis on downwind sailing ability.

All the competitors start together from the start line and sail three laps of the course. The first board across the finish line is the winner of that race. An Olympic competition normally consists of seven races and the winner is the competitor with the best six out of seven results.

Funboard Racing

Funboard racing is the term used to describe racing that takes place in winds of over 11 knots at world tour and production board events. The three disciplines included are course racing, slalom racing and wave performance.

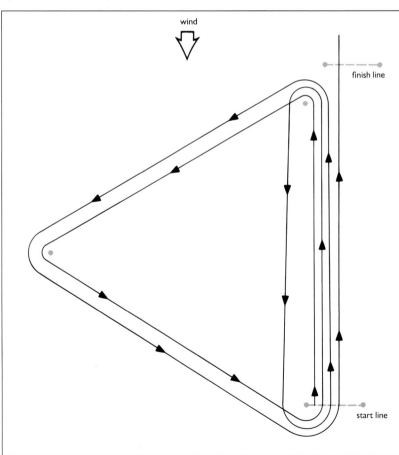

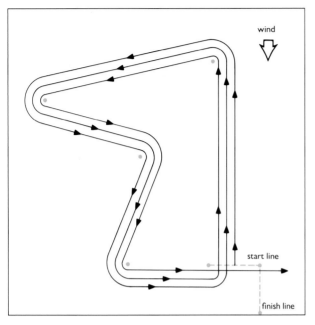

Fig 98   The new Olympic course.

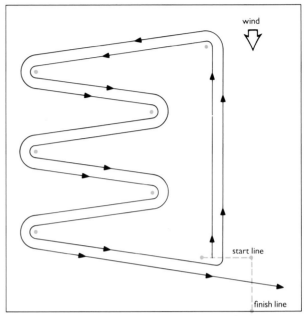

Fig 99   The funboard course racing course.

Course Racing

Course racing has developed from the original discipline of triangle racing and is the discipline most often raced in funboard competitions because it is not dependent on a specific wind direction. The type of course used consists of a beat followed by a series of long reaches and gybes. As with Olympic racing, all the competitors start together and the first person across the finish line is the winner of the race (Fig 99).

In winds of under 20 knots, competitors use course racing boards which are approximately 370cm (145in) long, 65cm (25in) wide and weigh approximately 13kg (30lb). In winds of over 20 knots large slalom boards are used as they are so much faster on the reaches. The sails used for course racing are all camber induced and most competitors will have a quiver of course racing sails ranging from 5.0–7.5 sq m (54–80 sq ft).

Slalom Racing

This is one of the most exciting windsurfing disciplines to watch.

Competitors start together in heats of eight to ten and then proceed around a tight course consisting of lots of reaching and gybing. The first person to cross the finish line is the winner. The course can either be a two-buoy course where the competitors start and finish in the same area and sail a figure-of-eight course (Fig 100), or it can be a downwind six-buoy slalom course (Fig 101).

Fig 100   The two-buoy slalom course.

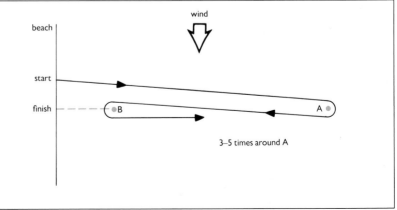

STAR TIP

If you get a good start in a slalom race you have the best chance of winning. When you leave the line clear in front you have all the wind you want.

Bjorn Dunkerbeck
Boards, 52, 1988.

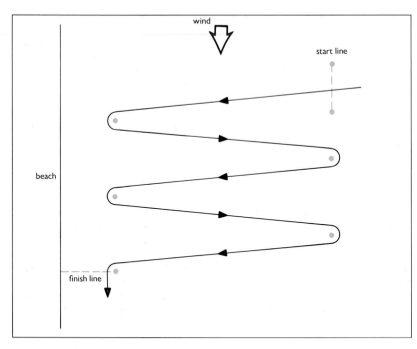

Fig 101   The six-buoy downwind slalom course.

If there are a large number of competitors, the competition is sailed in heats with the winners of each heat going through to the next round. A board used in slalom competitions is normally 260–290cm (100–115in) long depending on the wind strength and the size of the rider. The rigs used are the same camber-induced sails as those used for course racing.

Wave Performance

Wave performance is similar to freestyle in that the competitors are marked by a panel of judges. The competitors sail in 8-minute heats of between two and four people. The winners go through to the next round and this continues until there is an overall winner. The judges mark the competitors on wave riding, jumping and transitions. Boards that are used for this type of event are normally specifically designed for the sailor's weight and style. Most wave boards are 240–260cm (95–100in) long. Generally the smaller boards are more manoeuvrable in big waves and

strong winds. If the wind is not constant larger boards are used.

The sails used have much shorter booms than sails used for other disciplines and they do not have camber inducers. They mostly have a dual-batten system which allows the choice of either full or half-length battens. In general wave sails are very light and manoeuvrable, but not as powerful as the sails used in other disciplines.

Some of the tricks commonly performed in wave competitions are:

1.   The duck gybe – a normal carve gybe but in this case with the sail passing over your head instead of over the front of the board.
2.   The 360-degree turn – this is a turn that begins as a normal carve gybe, but the board continues through 360 degrees until you are back to where you started.
3.   An upside-down jump – you take off from a wave and kick the board over your head so that you are hanging upside-down from the booms.
4.   The forward loop – this is a very

advanced manoeuvre. You take off on a wave and then roll forward to spin your board and rig through a complete loop to land safely!
5.   The cutback – this is a sharp turn made at the top of a wave which takes you down the front of the wave to the point where it is breaking.
6.   The bottom turn – this is a sharp turn made at the bottom of a wave to take you back up to the top.

Your First Competition

Many people who windsurf continually believe that they are not good enough to race until at last they get bullied into entering, are surprised at how much they enjoy it, and then are upset that they have been missing out for so many years. As I mentioned previously, there is organised racing for every level of competitor. The best place to start is at club level, and if you find you are doing well here you will probably meet others who are competing in the national circuit. Once on the national circuit you can qualify for international races, and then you might be on your way to the Olympics or World Cup!

KEY POINT

- Arrive in plenty of time to prepare yourself for your first race.
- Don't be intimidated by others on the water – you have as much right to be there!
- Don't be demoralized if you finish last – you probably won't, but everyone has to start somewhere and somebody always has to be last!

Once you have mastered the basics of windsurfing you are ready to race at club level, in fact there is no better way to improve. As long as you are in control of your board and able to keep out of the way of others there is no reason why you should not enter a club race.

Entering your first race can be a

daunting prospect, so an explanation follows of the things you need to know, what to expect and how to go about it all.

RULES CHECK

A board on starboard tack has right of way over a board on port tack. You are on starboard tack when your right arm is nearest the mast; port tack is when your left arm is nearest the mast.

Sail Numbers

Find out from your local club or shop when the next race is, what the start times are, and if you need to pay an entry fee. Sail numbers are used for identification purposes – you will need a sail number

later on in your racing career if not now. If you join the national association they will tell you what your sail number is and this will be your sail number for life if you continue to renew your membership. The association will be able to sell you the number – this is made from sticky-back fablon and you need one set of numbers for each side of the sail. (If you are likely to use more sails you will also need numbers for those.)

Applying Sail Numbers

To stick the numbers on, unroll your sail in a clean, dry and obstacle-free area. Dry and clean the area where the numbers are to go (see Fig 102). Place a piece of flat board under this panel, and lay the numbers out on the sail so that you are sure of the spacing and know that you can fit them all in. Peel off a 2.5cm (1 in) section

of backing from your first number. Stick the corner of this number on to the sail, press down and then peel off the rest of the backing a little at a time, pressing down the sail number as you go. Continue this method for the remaining numbers – if you have a 6, 8 or 0 in your number you will find it easiest to cut the number in half and then stick it on. Press the numbers down firmly once they are on the sail.

Insurance

It is a very good idea to have insurance whether you race or not. Most clubs insist that all members are covered in case they injure somebody – this is called third party insurance. If you join the RYA they will give you free third party insurance. If you own good quality windsurfing equipment it is worthwhile getting it insured against theft and damage.

Now that you know when the race is and have a sail number and insurance, all you need is to get to the start line on time.

Race Day

Aim to arrive at the club with plenty of time to spare before the race – at least one hour before, depending on how long it takes you to get rigged up and changed.

There will normally be a briefing about a half-hour before the scheduled start of the race. Make sure that you are ready to go on the water as soon as it has finished. If you have to sign on and/or pay an entry fee, remember to do this before the briefing.

Briefing

At the briefing you will be told about the course. It will normally be drawn on a blackboard – if there is anything that you don't understand, ask the person giving the briefing. If the course is complicated, draw yourself a diagram on your hand. Make sure you know what the start sequence is. Hooters will normally go off at 6- and 3-minute intervals so that you

Fig 102 Positioning the sail numbers.

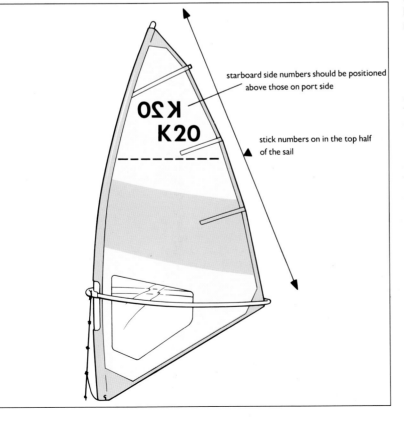

starboard side numbers should be positioned above those on port side

stick numbers on in the top half of the sail

Fig 103   Anders Bringdal course racing his Tiga board.

Fig 104   Gybe mark action during a course race.

can set your watch and know how long you have until the start.

On the Water

As soon as the briefing is over, get on to the water, and if possible sail the course so that you familiarize yourself with the sailing area. Work out where the start line is and make sure you are near it when the

RULES CHECK

In most races if you hit a mark you must perform a 720-degree penalty turn.

3-minute hooter goes. Set your watch so that you know you have 3 minutes to go until the start.

As this is your first race you will probably want to keep out of the way of the crowd at the start line. Most people try to start at either one end or the other of the line and there is usually a large gap in the middle – you should start here.

Use your watch to make sure that you cross the start line as the start gun goes, and then off you go!

PART 3
SAFETY

CHAPTER 11

SAFETY FOR THE WINDSURFER

Windsurfing is a very safe sport. There have not been many accidents and those that occur are normally because the windsurfer was unaware of potentially dangerous conditions or of how to rescue himself or herself. Here we will look at the methods of self-rescue so that if you do get into trouble you will know how to get yourself out of it!

RULES CHECK

- Always check the weather forecast before going windsurfing.
- Never sail on your own.
- Tell somebody that you are going out.
- Never sail in the dark or fog.
- Don't sail when you are tired.

However well prepared you are you may still find yourself in trouble one day – perhaps you will experience equipment failure or the weather will suddenly change. It is important to know how to rescue yourself and to practise so that you know what to do when you are in a panic situation. You can never rely on others to rescue you, as a windsurfer in the water is hardly visible from the shore – however hard you wave and shout it is possible that you won't be noticed. Below are some self-rescue techniques; note that they differ for long and short boards because of the differences in board volume.

It is advisable to wear a buoyancy aid when windsurfing. Most chest harnesses also act as a buoyancy aid, but you must wear a buoyancy aid with a seat harness as this will provide no flotation.

Long Board Self-Rescue

If you become overpowered or tired on a long board you can normally get back to shore just by holding the rig out in front of you – this only works if you need to go across the wind or downwind.

Self-Rescue Downwind or Across the Wind

1. To go across the wind, stand with your back to the wind and pull the rig up until the boom end is the only bit left in the water (*see* Fig 105).

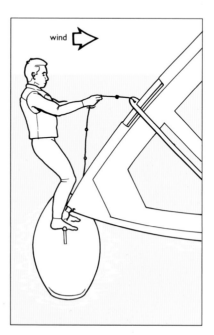

Fig 105   How to return to the shore across the wind if you become tired or overpowered.

KEY POINT

To work out where the wind is coming from, stand up and turn around slowly until you can feel the wind coming directly square on to your face so that it is blowing your hair straight back. You are now looking directly into the wind.

2. To go directly downwind, pull the rig completely clear of the water and turn to face the front of the board. Position the rig so it is also pointing over the front of the board (*see* Fig 106).

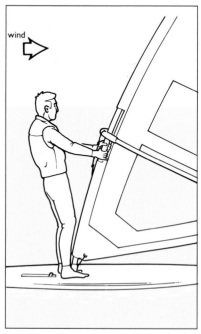

Fig 106   How to return to the shore downwind if you become tired or overpowered.

Fig 107   A controlled jump off a good wave.

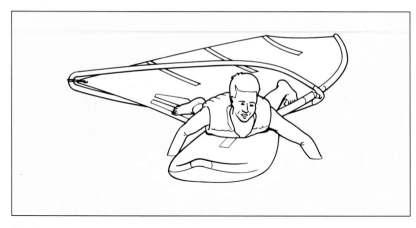

Fig 108   Paddling the board and rig back to shore if the wind drops.

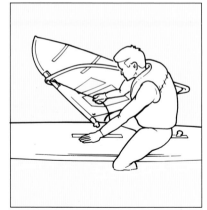

Fig 109 (a)   Sitting astride the board and undoing the mast foot and safety leash.

3.   If the wind dies completely you can get back to shore by pulling the rig over the back of the board and paddling, holding the rig in place with your feet (see Fig 108).

Self-Rescue Upwind
(Figs 109 (a)–(c))

However, if you need to go upwind to get back to the shore you will have to de-rig the sail, put it on the board and paddle back to the shore. This is time- and energy-consuming and not recommended if you are tired and cold.

1.   Sit astride your board and undo the mast foot and safety leash. Take out the battens and store them in the mast sleeve.
2.   Undo the outhaul and push the end of the boom up to the top of the sail. Roll the sail up tightly starting from the clew end until it is tight against the mast.

If your boom clamps on to the mast and will not fold up in line with it, use the following method:

a)   Undo the outhaul.
b)   Undo the uphaul and wrap it tightly around the mast just below the boom.

c)   Undo the boom clamp and fold the boom up against the mast.
d)   Roll the sail up tightly starting from the clew end until it is tight against the mast.

3.   Take the outhaul line and tie it around the top half of the mast and sail to keep them together. Take the uphaul and tie it around the bottom half of the sail and mast. Lay the rolled up rig across the board.
4.   Rotate the rig around underneath you so that it is in line with the board. You should have a towing eye attached to the

Fig 109 (b)   Undoing the outhaul, pushing the boom up against the mast and rolling the sail.

Fig 109 (c)   Securing the rig using the outhaul line around the top of the sail, and the uphaul around the bottom half of the sail and mast.

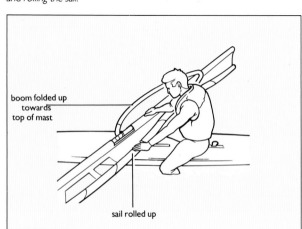

boom folded up
towards
top of mast

sail rolled up

boom

uphaul line

sail
wrapped
around mast

outhaul line
tying boom to mast

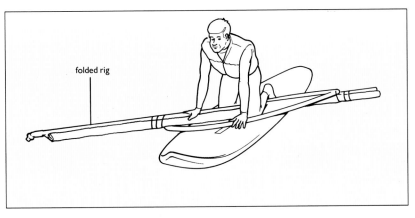

Fig 110   Rotating the rig underneath you so that it is in line with the board.

Fig 111   Lying on top of the rig and paddling to the shore.

front of the board – slide the mast foot through this.

5.   Lie on the board and paddle with your arms to the shore. You will have to take your harness off or turn it around so that the hook doesn't attack the board.

This type of self-rescue can be very tiring, and if you are already cold and tired do not attempt it; instead ditch your rig and paddle the board back to shore. You can then fetch help to rescue your rig – remember your life is more important. It is vital to make the decision to self-rescue as soon as you realise that you are in trouble. The longer you leave it the further you will be from shore.

Rescuing Others

(Fig 112)

If you come across someone in difficulty on the water and there is no one with a suitable rescue craft, you can try to tow them in. Tell them how to de-rig their sail for self-rescue as given above, and then position their board so that they are pointing towards the shore.

1.   Position your board and rig so that it is to leeward of the board in trouble. Tell the person to put his leeward hand around your mast foot and to hold firmly on to his board and rig with his other hand. Do not attempt to sail with him on

your leeward side or he will be hit on the head by your rig!

2.   Pull up your rig and start sailing. You will find that there is more pressure in the rig due to the extra drag. Take care not to step or fall on your survivor.

3.   If you have to tack upwind, remember to transfer your survivor to the windward side again.

Fig 112   Towing another windsurfer.

Short Board Self-Rescue

On a short board, rolling up your rig and paddling to safety is not so easy because of the lack of volume in the board. Over the page are some of the unfortunate situations that you may find yourself in along with some tried and tested solutions.

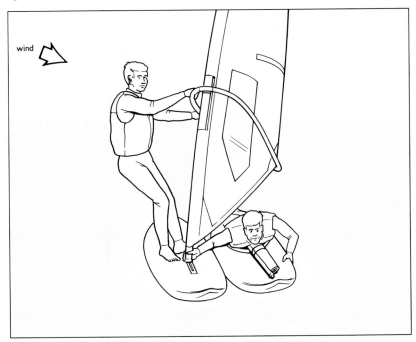

1.   One of the most common occurrences is for the universal joint to break. To get home safely here are two suggestions:

a)   Use the excess downhaul line to tie the mast base tightly to the star plate or similar fitting to which the UJ normally connects. You should now be able to waterstart and return to shore. The problem with this method is that the mast base and broken UJ can scrape your board quite badly. This is, however, better than losing your rig!

b)   You can try to paddle home by tying the rig to the back footstrap using the downhaul line and paddling the board forwards. This will be slow and hard work. If you are making little headway leave your rig and paddle the board in on its own – you can come back for the rig later with a boat.

2.   Another potential problem is that you run out of wind or break your skeg.
     If this happens the fastest way to paddle in is backwards, with the rig attached so that it is towed behind and to the side.

3.   One of the worst dilemmas is if your mast breaks. If you try to tow your rig it will probably sink because of the water entering the mast. The best thing to do is to de-rig the sail, leave the broken mast and paddle ashore with the boom and sail. However, you can get very cold and tired trying to de-rig in rough sea conditions, so if you are beginning to risk your life ditch the complete rig. Good insurance cover will buy you a new rig but not a new life!

Carrying Spares

You can avoid many potential problems by being aware of them and taking sensible precautions, such as carrying some spares. A good place to carry these is in a small 'bum-bag' worn on the lower back.
     Here are some spares suggestions:

1.   Rope for harness lines and so on.
2.   A knife for cutting line.
3.   A spare harness line holder.

4.   A small skeg for emergencies and a screwdriver.
5.   A spare UJ.
6.   A whistle.
7.   A day-glo flag.
8.   A flare pack.
9.   Change for a phone call if you come ashore down the coast, or for ice-creams.

Attracting Attention

If you cannot rescue yourself and need help here are some ways to attract attention:

1.   If someone is near enough to see you, wave your arms above your head (see Fig 113).
2.   Whistle or shout.
3.   Wave your day-glo flag above your head.
4.   Use your distress flares.

Fig 113   The distress signal.

Safety Guide-Lines

Below are some sensible safety guide-lines that can prevent you from needing to be rescued:

1.   Try to get an accurate wind and sea forecast before launching.
2.   Always sail with others and make sure that they are aware that you are there;

they will probably be just as glad to know that you will keep an eye out for them.
3.   Always tell someone that you are going out and when to expect you back. If you are totally alone, ring the coastguard when you go and when you return – they want to encourage more windsurfers to do this.
4.   Never sail in the dark or in fog.
5.   Don't sail for too long so that you are too exhausted to get back in that 'one last time'.

KIT CHECK

It is very important to carry a safety pack with you if you are going to be sailing away from the beach. Some examples of what you should carry are: a knife, rope, screwdriver, universal joint, whistle, day-glo flag, flares and money for a phone call.

Understanding Water and Wind

Tides

Strong tides can be an invisible danger to the ill-informed windsurfer. Every beach has its own peculiarities and the best way to find out about them is to ask experienced local windsurfers. You can normally buy specific tide-tables cheaply from a local newsagent. These will tell you the daily high and low tides and give you an idea of whether it is a strong or weak tide.
     If you do not have any tide-tables you can normally work out whether the tide is going in or out by looking at the beach. If the beach is dry the tide is coming in, and if the beach is wet the tide is going out (except if it is raining!). The tide normally works in a 6-hour cycle – it goes out for 6 hours and then comes in for 6 hours, with the strongest tide in the middle 2 hours of a cycle.
     At most beaches the tide will flow along the shore – find out from the locals which way it flows and then make allowances for this when you are sailing. Be careful not to end up downtide and downwind as you

will find it very hard to get home if the wind dies.

Rips

A rip is a very strong current that is normally found on surf beaches where the waves pound on to the beach – the tons of water need an escape route and this normally forms naturally as a channel. The water races rapidly out to sea through this channel and is in fact often used by surfers as a conveyor belt to speed them out to the breaks. If you get caught in one, don't panic! Let the rip take you out to sea and then start again from there, avoiding its path in future! Rips are best avoided, but if you do find yourself in one it is not worth the energy spent fighting against it – it will eventually stop and let you back in again.

Offshore Winds

An offshore wind is one that blows at approximately 60 degrees either side of straight out to sea.

Offshore winds are the most common cause of rescues and the simple answer is not to go out in them. Your local beach might look idyllically flat and just right for learning those new tricks, but don't be deceived. The wind will be gusty and unstable, the further you go out to sea the stronger it will get, and you have no safety net in an offshore wind – just a distant shore!

Fig 114   John Dickens in flight at Kimmeridge Bay.

CHAPTER 12

CARE OF EQUIPMENT

Looking after your equipment properly can play an important part in your safety. If it is maintained in good order and is constantly checked you will be able to avoid equipment failure out at sea – this is the cause of a large percentage of rescues. Here is a check-list to help you take care of your gear:

1. Always replace frayed lines – from your harness, inhaul, outhaul and downhaul.
2. Wash out booms thoroughly with fresh water immediately after use. Also wash your sail, mast and board. When rinsing the board pay particular attention to the mast track and centreboard casing.
3. Check your mast foot after every sail. Tighten any nuts that are coming loose and replace the rubber section if it is worn or cracked.
4. Check your masts for any cracks around the boom area and the base.
5. Check the boom end fittings for cracks and check that the rivets are secure.
6. Try always to keep your equipment under cover when it is not in use so that it is not damaged by light.

KIT CHECK

If your equipment is maintained in good order and is constantly checked, you will be able to avoid equipment failure which is the main reason for rescues.

Travelling with your Equipment

This is another area where you have to be aware of the potential hazards both to your equipment and to other people. If a board is not tied on properly, or a roof-rack not firmly attached to the car, you can lose your load and cause serious injury or death to other road users. Some safety measures you can take are:

1. Always check your roof-rack to make sure that it is not coming loose from the car.

Fig 115 Windsurfing equipment needs to be securely strapped to your car.

2. Check your roof-rack straps to make sure that they are not about to break.
3. Tie a retaining strap from the front of the board down to the front bumper of the car to prevent the board from lifting off the car.
4. Tie your equipment on as in Fig 115.

To take care of your equipment when travelling, use bags to prevent knocks and

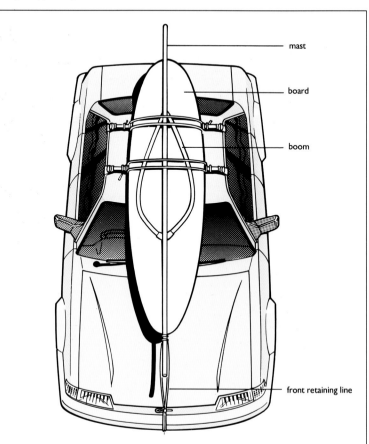

mast

board

boom

front retaining line

to protect against road dirt which will affect your board. It is easy to get a stone chip and not notice it. This will then cause your board to leak – board bags can prevent this. You can buy special bags for your boards, masts, sails and booms. These are particularly useful when travelling by air.

KIT CHECK

To take care of your equipment when travelling, use bags to prevent knocks and stop road dirt damaging your board.

Looking after your Wetsuit

If your wetsuit is to continue keeping you warm and safe from hypothermia you will have to look after it and treat it with respect. A wetsuit that is left wet and sandy in the back of a car between outings will soon begin to delaminate and stink! Always wash your wetsuit out with fresh water after every sail and hang it up to dry inside out so that the colours do not fade.

Once your wetsuit is dry, store it in a dry place away from direct sunlight as this also will cause the neoprene to delaminate. Try always to hang your

wetsuit and not fold it. If you have to fold it, do so loosely so that you do not crease the neoprene – if a wetsuit is creased the neoprene can be damaged. When you are carrying your wetsuit, use a large hold-all to minimise creasing – try to find a hold-all with a separate dry compartment so that the suit can be kept away from your dry clothes.

Wetsuit boots should be treated in a similar fashion – rinse after use and store somewhere dry and away from direct sunlight. Some makes of wetsuit boot are prone to smelling! If yours do begin to smell try soaking them outside in an antiseptic solution.

Fig 116   Performing a pirouette whilst sailing the board on its rail.

PART 4
FITNESS

CHAPTER 13

GENERAL FITNESS

Windsurfing is not a sport that demands an incredible level of fitness. Most windsurfers don't train on land, not even the professionals – they can keep their level of fitness high by windsurfing every day. That is fine if you live where there is constant wind. If you don't, or if you have to work five days a week and can only windsurf at weekends, you will benefit from a fitness training programme.

Why do you need to be fit for windsurfing? If you are not as fit as you could be, you will notice that on windy days you are the one sitting on the beach after a couple of hours of hard work, whilst the fit windsurfers are on the water enjoying themselves all day. As soon as you begin to get tired your skill level will also deteriorate. Increased fitness delays fatigue and enables you to maintain skill levels for longer periods of time. You will therefore be able to learn faster and have the satisfaction of being a better sailor.

Windsurfing in general requires the following:

1.   Good upper body strength to be able to handle strong gusts.
2.   Endurance to be able to stay out on the water all day when the conditions are good.
3.   Flexibility so that you can perform tricky manoeuvres and wipe out at speed without hurting yourself.
4.   A good cardio-vascular system, particularly for wave sailing and carrying your board up long beaches.

In this chapter I will look at ways to improve your general level of health and fitness, and include some specific exercises which have been designed with the windsurfer in mind. Also I discuss how to test your fitness and how to prevent spending hours off the water because of

STAR TIP

On physical fitness: *Sailing plays a very large part. I believe that hours spent on the water will prepare you better than hours spent running around the woods.*
Anders Bringdal
Boards, 54, 1988.

unnecessary injury. But first a word of caution – do not start any strenuous fitness training programme before consulting your doctor.

Before doing any sort of fitness exercise it is important to warm up properly.

The Warm-Up

Warming up consists of a series of light, relaxed exercises. Their purpose is to raise muscle temperature, increase the effectiveness of muscular contraction and also give a general boost to the cardio-respiratory condition of the body. A good warm-up will result in a body that is better prepared for activity, and the risk of injury is lessened. It is also important to warm down with light exercise after a strenuous session. Do not allow your muscles to get cold suddenly.

Below are some suggestions for a light warm-up programme which should last for approximately 5 minutes:

1.   Jog loosely on the spot, keeping your toes in contact with the ground. Gently loosen up your whole body.
2.   Chest stretches – stand with your feet together, raise your arms forwards to stretch up and then drop them down to the side again. Repeat this 4 times.
3.   Side stretches – stand with your feet apart, put one hand on your head and lean

over to the other side. Reach down your leg as far as possible with your other hand and hold this stretched position for 3 seconds. Return to the start position and lean to the other side. Stretch 4 times to each side.
4.   Twists – stand with your feet apart and twist to the right. Hold this position for 3 seconds and then twist to the left and hold for 3 seconds. Twist 4 times to each side.
5.   Back arches – arch backwards as far as possible and hold for 3 seconds. Return to the start position and repeat 4 times.
6.   Toe reaching – stand with your feet together and slide your hands down your shins, then press your knees back and drop your head. Hold this position for 3 seconds, release and repeat 4 times.
7.   Shoulder pressing – stand with your feet and arms apart. Press your arms backwards and hold for 3 seconds. Release and repeat 4 times.
8.   Shoulder stretching – stand with your feet apart, stretch your arms up and hold for 3 seconds. Release and repeat 4 times.
9.   Ski bounces – standing with your feet apart and arms out at your side to help you balance, swing into a squat position and then stand again having swung your arms behind you. Swing down again and back into your original position, keeping your seat low with a full knee bend on the forward and back swings. Repeat 4 times.
10.   Side swings – stand with your feet apart and both arms in the air out to one side. Swing into a deep squat and then out with your arms to the other side. Repeat 4 times.
11.   Lunges – stand with your legs wide astride and your right leg directly in front of your left leg. Point your right foot forwards with your left foot turned to point outwards. Keep your rear leg straight and bend the knee of your front

Fig 117   Sailing on a tandem board in light winds.

leg to lower your trunk into a deep lunge position. Push back to straighten your front leg and return to a standing position. Repeat this 4 times before changing over so that your left leg is in front.

Cardio-Vascular Fitness

Once you have warmed up, a good way to improve your endurance and cardio-vascular system is to put your heart under pressure for at least 20 minutes (preferably 30–40 minutes) each day for 6 days per week. There are various forms of exercise suitable for this; they include running, swimming and cycling. Swimming and cycling are better exercises for your joints but running is the easiest way to put your heart under constant pressure for the necessary length of time.

The longer your heart is put under pressure, the better your endurance will be. Make a note of how long the run takes and try to improve on this daily. After the run measure your pulse rate – the time it takes to return to normal after exercise is a good guide to your fitness level. Take your pulse rate for 15 seconds after your run and multiply it by 4, then take it again 90 seconds later. The faster it returns to normal, the fitter you are.

Body Fitness

A good way to improve your body strength is to complete a circuit of activities which exercise all parts of the body by overloading different muscle groups in turn. The exercises given below need only a minimum of apparatus so they can be done anywhere.

1.   Modified press-ups – start with your hands resting on a sturdy chair or a bench and shoulder-width apart. Bend your arms until your chest touches the chair or bench whilst keeping your body straight. Push up so you are back in the starting position.

2.   Sit-ups – lie on your back with your hands crossed in front of your body and tucked under your armpits. Have your legs slightly bent and your feet tucked under a heavy piece of furniture or a radiator. Sit up so that your elbows touch your knees and then return to the starting position.

3.   Squats – start in a standing position. Squat to rest on your haunches and then return to the starting position.

4.   Back lifts – lie face down on the floor. Gently arch backwards using your hands to raise your head and shoulders off the ground as far as possible. Hold and then lower your body back to the floor to start again.

5.   Squat thrusts – start in the press-up position with your hands on the floor and legs fully extended (the hands remain in the same position throughout this exercise). Spring forwards to land with your knees level with your arms and then jump back to return your legs to the fully extended position. This counts as 1 squat thrust.

6.   Step-ups – stand in front of a bench, chair or stair which is between 45–50cm (18–20in) high. Step up on to the bench with your leading leg, fully extend it at the knee joint and lift the other leg up on to the stair. Step down again into the start position.

Alternate the leading leg each time you do this exercise.

Working out Your Programme

Complete a record card as shown below:

1.   Work through these exercises in order (it is important to stick to this order as it does not work any one muscle group in succession) doing as many repetitions of each exercise as possible in 30 seconds. Record your total for each exercise and then divide it by 2 to calculate your training number.

2.   Complete the exercise circuit 3 times at the training rate. It is important not to have a break between exercises so that you continually put your heart under pressure.

3.   Record the time taken for the total period of exercise on the record card. Every month you should review your training number – as your fitness improves you will be able to do more repetitions of each exercise in 30 seconds. You should try to do your circuits 3 times each week.

Activity	Maximum no. in 30 seconds	Training number
1. Press-ups 2. Sit-ups 3. Squats 4. Back lifts 5. Squat thrusts 6. Step-ups		
Date: Time: Improvement:		

CHAPTER 14

WEIGHT TRAINING

Another way to improve your strength is to train with light weights. Weight training gives you dynamic strength which is required mostly in wave sailing when you want to pull off a radical manoeuvre without using your harness.

The exercises listed below will build up your strength for the weight programme given in the next section. For the following exercises you will need a set of dumb-bells. Dumb-bells are light weights that you should grip in each hand when you do these exercises.

1. Sideways arm raise – stand facing forwards with your arms outstretched, raise them above your head and then return them to their original position.
2. Alternate upwards arm punching – stand facing forwards with your arms and elbows tucked into your chest and then punch upwards.
3. Twists – stand with your arms straight down at your sides. Twist as far around as you can (keeping your feet stationary on the floor). Return to the start position and twist the opposite way.
4. Side lifts – lean forwards so that your body is a right angle and your arms are hanging straight down. Lift your arms as high as possible and then return to the start position.
5. Alternate forwards punching – stand facing forwards with your arms bent at your sides and punch forwards.
6. Alternate curls – hold your arms out straight in front of you with your palms up. Curl one hand towards you, bending only at the wrist. Repeat with the other arm.

Make a record card out as below to record the maximum number of each exercise that you can perform in 30 seconds. Divide this number by 2 to arrive at your training number and then do 3 sets

Activity	Maximum no. in 30 seconds	Training number	No. of sets
1. Sideways arm raise			3
2. Alternate upwards arm raise			3
3. Twists			3
4. Side lifs			3
5. Alternate forwards punching			3
6. Alternate curls			3

of each exercise at this rate. This circuit should be done 3 times each week.

Heavier Weight Training

Upper body strength is very important for the windsurfer and there are very few sports that can build it up in such a way as weight training. The following exercises utilise a barbell which is a simple bar with weights on each end. Weight training can also be done in a properly equipped gymnasium where there is qualified instruction and supervision – this is preferable as lifting weights can be dangerous if not done properly. Weight training exercises that are particularly applicable to the windsurfer are:

1. Biceps curl – using an undergrasp grip, lift the barbell to the thigh support position. Keep your upper arm motionless and close to the body, then bend your elbows to curl the barbell to your chest, keeping your body upright. Make sure that your elbows are kept still and close to

your body throughout the curl. Hold for 1 second and then let the barbell back down.
2. Press behind neck – lift the bar and place it in the shoulder rest position. Keep your hands just slightly more than shoulder-width apart with your feet parted sideways and flat on the floor. Push the barbell overhead until your elbows lock and then lower to repeat the exercise.
3. High-pulls – start from the crouch position, holding the bar in an overhead grip. Drive hard with your legs and rise on to your toes whilst pulling the bar to your chin in one continuous movement. In the final position your legs should be fully extended with your arms out to the side and your elbows flexed. Lower the barbell to the floor and repeat.
4. Squat – hold the bar with an overhand grip in the chest rest position. Your feet should be comfortably apart with your hands just slightly more than shoulder-width apart. Bend your hips and knees to lower your trunk and the barbell

until your thighs are almost parallel to the floor. From this position push upwards by straightening your hips and knees and resume the standing position.

5.   Wrist curl – hold the barbell with an underhand grip with your hands about shoulder-width apart. Sit on a bench with the back of your forearms resting on the front of your thighs. Your feet should be flat on the floor. Extend your wrist fully, allowing the barbell to roll as far as possible on to your fingers. Without moving your forearms, curl your wrists to a maximum contraction by flexing your fingers and wrists. Lower the barbell to the start position and repeat.

6.   Reverse wrist curl – this time hold the barbell with an overhand grip and repeat the above exercise.

7.   Pull-over – lie flat on your back on a bench with your head supported, trunk

Exercise	No. of reps	No. of sets
1. Biceps curl	10	3
2. Press behind neck	10	3
3. High pulls	10	3
4. Squat	10	3
5. Wrist curl	10	3
6. Reverse wrist curl	10	3
7. Pull-over	10	3

and hips straddling the bench and your feet flat on the floor. Place the barbell on the floor at the head of the bench. Reach out and take hold of the bar with an overgrasp grip and lift it to rest on your chest. Try to keep your elbows at right angles and raise the barbell up over your head and lower to the starting position.

Above is a chart showing the number of repetitions and sets that you should start with for each exercise. As you progress you will want to increase this.

Fig 118   You need to be strong to perform advanced manoeuvres such as this aerial gybe.

CHAPTER 15

SPECIFIC FITNESS TRAINING FOR THE WINDSURFER

The best training for windsurfing is definitely windsurfing! One of the best ways of finding out which muscles you need to work on is to make a note of the muscles that are hurting after a good day's windsurfing.

In the rest of this chapter I describe exercises that will improve your windsurfing. There are probably many more – if you can't find an exercise to suit your particular ache then try consulting an expert at your local gymnasium.

As I have previously mentioned it is imperative to warm up before any exercise. When you are going out from the beach on a cold day follow the warm-up schedule as prescribed on pages 112–14. You may feel silly doing this in your wetsuit on the beach, but not half as stupid as you would look with torn ligaments or damaged muscles for 6 weeks or longer.

If you are competing you will often find that you are either sent out on the water quite a while before the start of the race or have to wait for another race to finish before you start. In this case it is important to do a quick warm-up programme on the water.

On-the-Water Warm-Up for Windsurfers

1. Sit on your board and do some rapid shadow boxing.
2. Arm circling – sit on your board and circle each arm forwards and then back.
3. Do hand and neck circling in both directions.
4. Sit and put your legs straight out in front of you and touch your toes.
5. Rotate your feet.
6. Extend your ankles.
7. Stand up and hold the rig. Twist around as far as you can to either side.
8. Stand on your toes, whilst holding the rig.
9. Still holding your rig, do some light jogging, keeping your toes on the board.

Dry-Land Training

1. Hanging from a boom – you can imitate your sailing stance in your own living room by hanging an old boom from the ceiling – or if you are fussy about your decorations you could have it in the garage or garden. Suspend the boom at shoulder height with some rope and strong hooks, and hang from it in your usual stance – but without your harness! Turn on the telly or the Naish video and there you are. Time yourself and try to improve on the length of time that you can hang on next time. Change grips each time you do this exercise so that you use different muscles.
2. Pull-ups – for this exercise you need a strong beam or bar at about waist height. Lie on your back underneath the bar and reach up for it. If you can't reach, take hold of the bar first and then drop down underneath it so that your body and arms are straight. Now pull yourself up to the bar using only your arms until your chin reaches the bar, then drop down again. Do as many pull-ups as you can and try to improve on this number the next time you do them.
3. Hanging – find a strong bar that you can just reach with your arms extended above your head. Grab hold of the bar and lift your feet off the ground. Stay hanging from the bar for as long as you can. Try to improve your time the next time you do this exercise.

CHAPTER 16

FLEXIBILITY

Good flexibility will help you to be a better windsurfer. It will allow you to stretch further, it will be easier to try new manoeuvres and it will also lessen the possibility of injuries which can keep you off the water for lengthy periods. Flexibility training ensures that the complete range of movement is possible for each of the major joints and muscles – this reduces the chance of muscle and joint injury. The following exercises should be performed in a relaxed manner, with the range of movement gently increased each time. Never use sharp movements and stop if the exercise is painful.

1. Foot extension – sit on the floor with your legs together and pointing straight ahead. Tense your thigh muscles and press your toes and feet forwards until fully extended. Hold for 3 seconds and then release. Repeat this 4 times.
2. Foot rotation – sit on the floor with your legs together and pointing straight ahead. Tense your thigh muscles and rotate your feet clockwise 4 times and then anti-clockwise 4 times.
3. Foot contraction – start in the same position as for the previous exercises. Pull your feet and toes towards you, hold for a slow count of 3 and then release. Repeat this 4 times.
4. Alternate leg raising – lie flat on the floor with your legs together and pointing straight ahead. Stretch your right foot and raise your right leg as high as possible, hold for 3 seconds and then repeat with the other leg. Repeat this exercise 4 times with each leg.
5. Knee to chest contraction – lie flat on the floor with your legs together and tensed, pointing straight ahead. Lift your

right knee to your chest and keep your resting leg tensed. Press your knee down, hold for 3 seconds and release. Repeat this 4 times with each leg.
6. Knee presses – sit on the floor with the soles of your feet together. Press your knees down towards the floor, hold for 3 seconds and release. Repeat this 4 times.
7. Body raising – stand with your feet together and flat on the floor with your toes pointing forwards. Extend your feet until you are balanced on your toes and have raised your body. Hold for 3 seconds and release. Repeat 4 times.
8. Lunges – stand with your legs apart, turn your body sideways and turn your front foot to face the same way as your head. Keep your legs tensed and your arms held out to balance yourself. Lower your body into a lunge position by bending your front knee. Hold for 3 seconds and then release. Return to the starting position and repeat 4 times on each leg.
9. Shoulder press – stand up with your legs apart and arms straight out at your side. Press your arms and shoulders back, keeping your arms straight. Hold for 3 seconds and then release. Repeat 4 times.
10. Shoulder stretch – stand up with your legs apart and your arms straight up above your head. Stretch your shoulders and arms upwards for 3 seconds and then release.
11. Backwards stretch – stand up with your legs apart, arms above your head and bent at the elbows. Bend your arms and reach down your back as far as possible. Hold for 3 seconds and then release. Repeat this 4 times.
12. Back and leg extension – sit upright on the floor with your legs stretched apart. Slide your hands forward on the

floor between your legs. Keep your legs as far apart as possible and hold them tensed for 3 seconds and then release. Repeat 4 times.
13. Back and leg extension with twist – sit upright on the floor with your legs stretched apart. Reach with your hands towards your left ankle keeping your legs tensed. Hold this position for 3 seconds and then release. Do the same thing for your right ankle. Repeat this exercise 4 times on each side.
14. Back arches – lie face down on the floor with your hands directly below your shoulders. Push up on your hands to arch your back and chest, keeping your trunk on the floor. Hold for 3 seconds and then release. Repeat this exercise 4 times.
15. Plié – stand with your heels together and legs tensed, keeping your feet flat on the floor. Lower your trunk by bending your knees and pressing down directly over your feet. Hold for 3 seconds and then release, repeat 4 times.
16. Trunk twists – stand upright with your legs apart and hands clasped together behind your back. Twist your trunk to the right to look behind you, hold for 3 seconds and then release. Repeat 4 times on both sides.
17. Side leans – stand upright with your legs apart. Place your right hand on your head and lean over to the left side to reach as far down your left leg as possible with your left hand. Hold for 3 seconds and then release. Repeat 4 times on each side.

The best time to do these exercises is when you are warm, perhaps after a good day on the water. Try to do the flexibility programme 6 days each week.

CHAPTER 17

INJURY PREVENTION

If you follow the advice this book gives for preparing your body for windsurfing, you should be able to avoid most of the common windsurfing injuries. Below are some of the most common injuries with advice on exactly how they can be prevented.

The Back

This used to be the most common injury and cause of pain amongst windsurfers in the days when twisted light wind stances were popular, harnesses were poorly designed and boards weighed much more than they do now. The cumulative effect of the above caused a number of back problems unsurprisingly. Nowadays all such back pain should be avoidable – below are some typical back-breaking windsurfing habits with some tips on how they can be avoided.

1. Lifting your board off the car. Always bend your knees and not your back when you are lifting – better still get somebody else to help you.
2. Uphauling the sail. Make sure you are using the correct technique for this – keep your back straight and knees bent (*see* page 32).
3. Wearing a bad harness. Make sure your harness is both designed well and fits well as your lower lumbar spine needs to be well supported. Always try on a harness before you buy it.
4. Using too big a sail. Don't try to go out with too big a sail. You will end up twisting, pushing and pulling on your back while trying to handle the power. Don't do it if it is unnecessary.
5. Sailing on the same tack for too long. This can also cause back strain and the resulting problems. Tack as often as possible to keep the strain evenly balanced.
6. Lifting and carrying your board. Do not attempt to carry your board and sail together for long distances – you will either damage your back or your board! Carry them separately it might take more time but at least you will be able to go out again the next day!

To help to prevent any back injuries you can attempt to strengthen your back. Use those exercises specifically designed to that effect: the sit-up and back lift exercises described on page 114.

Ankles and Knees

After backs, ankles and knees are the most common area for injury. The majority of injuries occur when sailing in shallow water and when using footstraps that are the wrong size.

1. Sailing in shallow water. This doesn't sound like a dangerous thing to do – in fact it would seem very sensible not to go out of your depth! However, if you step off thinking that the water is deep and unexpectedly find that it only comes up to your knees, you can cause your ankles and knees serious injury. These injuries are normally ligament or muscle strains which can keep you off the water for several weeks.
2. Footstrap injuries. If your footstrap is too large you will find that your foot slides right through and it becomes hard to pull it out of the strap when you want to gybe or bail out from a jump. Set up your footstraps so that your feet will just go into them up to the first third and no further. Whilst on the subject of footstraps, also make sure that all the screws are well secured and covered so that they cannot pierce your feet!

CHAPTER 18

MENTAL TRAINING AND THE INNER GAME

So far in this book I have explained how to windsurf in most conditions and how to prepare your body so that you are fit enough to enjoy the sport. However, I have not mentioned much about the mental side of learning or competing.

You may well have read *The Inner Game of Tennis* by Timothy Gallwey (Jonathan Cape Ltd., 1975), or books along a similar theme. His book has changed the way we now think about approaching sports. Tim Gallwey's theory states that our bodies can learn new techniques instinctively if left to do so – it is only when our self-doubting minds enter the scene that we come up against problems. In his book he suggests ways to try to overcome this phenomenon by getting our body and mind to work together, as happens when we achieve our best results.

What is the Inner Game?

The inner game is the battle that goes on inside your body when you try to learn or complete a manoeuvre. Gallwey suggests that we have two selfs and he calls these 'self one' and 'self two'. Self two is the doing part of us – in other words the part that can get on and do manoeuvres if it isn't hindered by self one. Self one is the interfering mind that tries to judge performances as good or bad and introduces such detrimental emotions as self-doubt and over-confidence.

This idea is perhaps best explained with the use of a windsurfing analogy. You have read the books, seen the video, had your lessons and are now trying to go wind-surfing for the first time on your own.

STAR TIP

Mental preparation is more important than anything else and confidence comes from within yourself: if you are happy with your body, your material and your preparation, then you should have confidence in yourself and that translates to winning.

Anders Bringdal
Boards, 54, 1988.

You have just pulled the sail out of the water and are about to start speeding along when self one appears on the scene and starts trying to tell self two what to do next.

Self one at this point tries to give many different instructions to self two, such as: 'Get into the secure position', 'Select a goal', 'Take your back hand off the mast', 'Move your back foot back, but keep it over the centre-line'!

Self two cannot take all this in, and splash! Self one then tells self two how stupid it is to fall in right in front of everybody and how it is useless at the sport and should never have thought of trying it. Self two begins to believe this and continues to fall off in the same spot all afternoon!

How the Inner Game can Help you with Learning to Windsurf

Tim Gallwey suggests that 'to self two a picture is worth a thousand words'. He means that, as is the case with children, you can learn a lot better from visual images than from words.

If you stop and think about your learning process you will remember that when you were a child you learned to walk without any instruction from others. You saw others walking, realized it was a more sensible way of getting around than on all fours and adopted it – in other words, self two taught itself to walk. As we get older our 'thinking mind' (self one) develops and tries to involve itself in the learning process, even though self two can manage perfectly well if it is left on its own! You will also have noticed how easy it is for children to pick up a new language whilst adults have to spend years having proper lessons! Children learn so quickly because they haven't started to interfere with their natural learning process – in other words self one has not yet developed into an interfering force!

The best way to learn how to windsurf is from a combination of a good book, a video, a good instructor and practice in safe surroundings. A normal lesson will take the format of on-land demonstration and practice and then on-the-water demonstration and practice, with video and verbal analysis of the day. Take each stage of windsurfing slowly, breaking each step down into easy-to-understand areas. Self two will learn from watching, listening, reading and then practising.

When it is your turn to try a manoeuvre, just sit quietly for a few minutes and visualize exactly what you are going to do. Go on the water and imitate your instructor, have confidence in self two to be able to perform the task – don't let self one tell self two what to do.

If you fail at your first attempt, ask your instructor to perform the exercise again, watch carefully and then close your eyes and visualize yourself doing exactly the

Fig 119   Action at the gybe mark during a women's course race.

same. Keep your confidence in self two – don't chastise it for failing the first time. Many people complain that they know what they are supposed to do but cannot do it – this is because they are not letting self two get on with it and instead are trying too hard with self one.

Once you have succeeded in completing a manoeuvre, spend some time repeating it so that you can feel how it should be done correctly – be aware of your body position and which muscles you are using. This will teach self two the timing that is needed, which is something that you cannot be told and can only learn through experience. Everytime a manoeuvre is performed, a slight impression is made in the cells of the brain, and when it is repeated often enough the impression becomes a groove. The groove is similar to that on a record, and repeating a manoeuvre frequently will increase the probability that you will repeat it correctly under pressure.

It is easier said than done to try to stop self one from interfering. The key to the inner game is first to 'park' self one and then later bring it back to help self two. To park self one and stop it from interfering, you need to give it something else on which to concentrate, such as the rhythm of your breathing or the sound of the water lapping against your board.

As you progress, self one can be used purely as a realistic observer of self two, to programme goals and suggest ways of improving without being judgmental. It is extremely important that self one is not judgmental. If, for example, self one says: 'I'm useless at this, I always fall in', self two will eventually begin to believe it and you

will fall in all the time. Self one just needs to look at the facts. A non-judgmental self one will have more time to be aware of everything that is going on.

One of the most important ideas behind the inner game is to just 'let things happen' and then experience what they feel like. Most importantly, enjoy learning to windsurf and do not worry about the past or future – in other words who will be impressed if you can do it or who won't talk to you if you can't! Concentrate on the present and let your body windsurf.

The Inner Game and Competition

In a competition many people are at an equal skill level, and the difference between winning and losing is in mental approach and attitude.

At this stage it is even more important that you put your confidence in self two and allow yourself to sail at a realistic level. It is very easy to become anxious and to try to instruct self two on what to do. Self two doesn't need these interruptions and is much better off on its own. Again you have to occupy self one so that it cannot interfere – perhaps concentrate on the front of your board as it chops through the water.

There is evidence to suggest that every athlete's peak performance is achieved when he or she is in a state of relaxed concentration – this is the mental state you are aiming for, it takes practice but is a very valuable art not just in competition but in all avenues of life. To achieve this

state you must make sure that self one does not start to judge your performance – if you do have a poor stance for instance, and if self one becomes active and interferes, it is wasting valuable energy resources and you cannot be aware of everything else that is going on.

To enjoy your competition do not judge your performance by results. If you do this you are relying on the performance of others over which you have no control. Judge your performance by how well you have sailed. If you made no mistakes and have sailed to the best of your ability then you can congratulate yourself. If you did make mistakes, analyse them, work out where you went wrong and visualise completing the course without any mistakes so that next time you will do better.

Many people make the mistake of putting themselves under extreme pressure when they are competing – this leads to mistakes being made and results in self one chastizing self two for being so stupid and then the inevitable downhill spiral occurs. You should not see competition as a way of proving that you are better than somebody else as this immediately means that you will think you are useless if you lose, and hence you put pressure on yourself. You should see competition merely as a way of improving and pushing yourself to your limits – there are more important things in life than just being a good windsurfer.

The secret to succeeding is not trying too hard. Allow self two to perform within its capabilities – and do not let self one interfere.

APPENDIX

The Beaufort Scale of Wind Force

Beaufort No.	General Description	Sea Criterion	Landman's Criterion	Limits of Velocity in knots
0	Calm	Sea like a mirror	Calm; smoke rises vertically	Less than 1
1	Light air	Ripples with the appearance of scales are formed, but without foam crests.	Direction of wind shown by smoke drift but not by wind vanes.	1 to 3
2	Light breeze	Small wavelets, still short but more pronounced. Crests have a glassy appearance and do not break.	Wind felt on face; leaves rustle; ordinary vane moved by wind.	4 to 6
3	Gentle breeze	Large wavelets. Crests begin to break. Foam of glassy appearance. Perhaps scattered white horses.	Leaves and small twigs in constant motion. Wind extends light flags.	7 to 10
4	Moderate breeze	Small waves becoming longer, fairly frequent white horses.	Raises dust and loose paper; small branches are moved.	11 to 16
5	Fresh breeze	Moderate waves, taking more pronounced long form; many white horses are formed. Chances of some spray.	Small trees in leaf begin to sway. Crested wavelets form on inland waters.	17 to 21
6	Strong breeze	Large waves, taking form; the white foam crests are more extensive everywhere. Probably some spray.	Large branches in motion; whistling heard in telegraph wires, umbrellas used with difficulty.	22 to 27
7	Near gale	Sea heaps up and white foam from breaking waves begin to be blown in streaks along the direction of the wind.	Whole trees in motion; inconvenience felt when walking against wind.	28 to 33
8	Gale	Moderately high waves of greater length; edges of crests begin to break into spin-drift. The foam is blown in well-marked streaks along the direction of the wind.	Breaks twigs off trees; generally impedes progress.	34 to 40
9	Severe gale	High waves. Dense streaks of foam along the direction of the wind. Crest of waves begin to topple, tumble and roll over. Spray may affect visibility.	Slight structural damage occurs (chimney-pots and slates removed).	41 to 47

GLOSSARY

Apparent wind   Wind that you feel when you are moving and that differs from true wind when you are standing still.

Battens   Glass fibre strips that slot into the sail to help create a more rigid profile.

Beach start   A way of starting in shallow water by stepping straight on to the board without using the uphaul.

Beating   Sailing the closest course possible to the wind.

Boom   The aluminium bar that encompasses the sail and attaches to the mast and clew of the sail.

Boom clamp   The clamp that connects the boom to the mast.

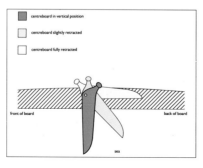

Bottom turn   This is a high speed turn made at the bottom of a wave. It is an advanced manoeuvre which requires much practice.

Bow   The front of the board.

Camber inducer   This is a piece of plastic that rotates around the mast. The batten slots into it and it gives the sail a better aerodynamic shape which is more efficient.

Carve gybe   A gybe performed in planing conditions with no centreboard. The board is turned by foot pressure and not by the sail.

Centreboard   Used on high volume boards to help them sail upwind; it is retracted into the board when going downwind in strong winds. It is sometimes called a daggerboard.

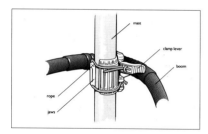

Cleat   A small fitting used to secure control lines.

Clew   The back corner of the sail that is attached to the end of the boom.

Close hauled   The course you sail when beating.

Concaves   A slight curving on the underside of boards which produces greater speed.

Course racing   A discipline of windsurfing which involves sailing around a large course marked by buoys. The course normally involves mainly upwind work.

Cut back   A wave sailing manoeuvre consisting of a sharp turn made at the top of a wave.

Downhaul   The line that controls the tension of the luff.

Duck gybe   A gybe similar to the carve gybe but where the boom passes over the head of the sailor instead of around the front of the board.

Duck tack   A tack which involves ducking under the sail – a freestyle manoeuvre.

Foot   The bottom of the sail.

Footstraps   Normally made of plastic and neoprene and can be adjusted to fit the size of your feet. They are firmly attached to the board and are normally used when reaching to stop your feet from being washed off the board.

Freestyle   A competitive discipline of windsurfing which involves the sailor performing tricks.

Funboard   A term used to describe a board that performs well in over 11 knots of wind.

Gate start   A method of starting a fleet of boards.

Gybe   Turning the board around away from the wind.

Harness   A device worn around the chest, waist or seat. It has a hook attached to it which connects to lines from the booms. This takes the strain off the sailor's arms.

Inhaul   A rope or clip that attaches the boom to the mast.

Leeward   The side of the board away from the wind.

Luff   The front of the sail.

To luff someone   To cause someone to head up into the wind.

Mast   A tapered fibreglass or aluminium tube that slides up inside the sail.

Mast extension   Used if the mast needs to be extended to fit a different sail.

Mast foot   The fitting that connects the mast to the board. It consists of a universal joint which enables the mast and sail to be turned and inclined in any direction.

Mast sleeve   The sleeve of the sail into which the mast fits.

Mast track   Allows the position of the mast foot to move up and down the length of the board.

Nose   Another term for the front of the board.

Planing   A term used to describe the motion of the board when it moves at sufficient speed to skim across the surface of the water rather than sail through it.

Port   Left – if your left hand is closest to the mast you are sailing on port tack.

Pumping   A term used to describe the rowing motion of the sail that can propel the board even when there is no wind.

Rail   The edge of the board.

Railriding   To sail on the side of the board – a freestyle trick.

Rig   A term used to describe the mast, boom and sail collectively.

Sail numbers   These are used for identification purposes in competitions.

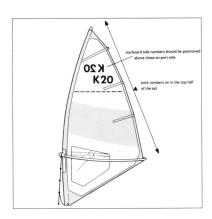

Sheeting in   To pull in on the boom with your back hand.

Skeg   Helps in the steering of the board. It is made of plastic, glass or carbon fibre. It fits into the skeg box on the undersurface of the board near the stern.

Spin-out   A problem that occurs when reaching at high speed. The skeg loses grip and the board starts to slide sideways.

Starboard   Right – if your right hand is closest to the mast you are on starboard tack.

Stern   A term used to describe the back area of the board.

Tail   Another term used to describe the back area of the board.

Tacking   Turning the board through the eye of the wind.

Transport   Your equipment must be securely strapped to your car when travelling.

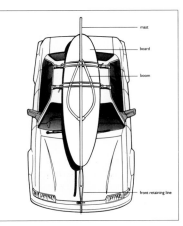

Trimming   Adjusting the board and sails to the conditions.

Uphaul   The thick rope used to pull the sail out of the water.

Uphauling   Pulling the sail out of the water using the uphaul rope.

Waterstart   A method of getting on to the board in deep water without uphauling.

Waves   You must choose the right wave if you want to jump.

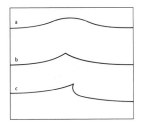

Wetsuit   A neoprene suit that keeps you warm in the water.

Window   The clear panel in the sail which allows you good visibility for obstacles and so on.

Windshift   A change in the wind direction.

Windward   The side of the board nearest the wind.

INDEX

Note Page numbers in *italics* refer to illustrations.

advanced board, *14*, 16
advanced rig, 17–18
aerial gybe, *69*

balancing, 30
batten, 12, 17
batten pocket, 12
beach start, 48
beginner's board, *10*, 10
beginner's rig, 17
board, 12, 13
boom, 12, 17
boom clamp, 12, 18
boom slot, 12
boots, 22
bottom turn, 88
buoyancy, 22
bow, 12
briefing, 97

camber inducer, *18*
carrying the board, 29–30
carve gybe, 70–1
centreboard, 12, 49
centreboard case, 12
centre of effort, 38–9
centre of lateral resistance, 38–9
chop hopping, 78
cleat, 12
clew, 12
close hauled course, 40–1
closing the gap, 69
clothing, 21–2
competition, 89, 96
composite, 13
construction, 13
course racing, 95
cut back, 88

downhaul, 12
downwind, 42–3
Drake, Jim, 10
drysuit, 21–2
duck gybe, 82–3

endurance, 112–14
flare gybe, 52
flares, 106

flexibility, 112, 118
foot, 12
foot steering, 50
foot strap, 12, 16, 46, 59
   beating straps, 59
   reaching straps, 60
freestyle, 89–93
funboard racing, 94

gloves, 22
gybing, 42–3
   on waves, 86–7

half-length battens, 18
harness, 53–5
harness lines, 54
hypothermia, 21

in-haul, 12
injury, 119
inner game, 120
insurance, 97
intermediate's board, 14–16
intermediate's rig, 17

jumping, 84–5

knockout freestyle, 89

landing, 86
launching, 26, 46–7, 83–4
learning, 23
long distance racing, 93
luff sleeve, 18

marathons, 93
mast, 12, 14
   extension, 12
   foot, 12, 58
   sleeve, 12
   socket, 12
   track, 12, 16
monofilm, 19
moving off, 36, *36–7*
mylar, 19

no-go zone, 39–40
nose, 12

Olympics, 51, 94

polyester, 19
polyethylene, 13
polystyrene, 13
polyurethane, 13
pumping, 72–4

racing rig, 18
rail, 12
reserve buoyancy, 16, 75
returning to beach, 44, 84
rig, 17
rigging up, 28–9
rig recovery, 62–3

sail, 17, 19, 44, 45
sail materials, 19
sail numbers, 97
Schweitzer, Hoyle, 10
second-hand board, 20
second-hand rig, 20
self-rescue, 102–6
shoes, 22
simulator, 23
size, 13–14
skeg, 12
skeg box, 12
slalom racing, 95
slam gybe, 81
spares, 106
speed sailing, 93, 94
spin out, 86
stance, 68
stern, 12
steering, 38, 48

sun, 22

tacking, 40–2
tacking a short board, 76
tail, 12
tandem freestyle, 93
tides, 106
towing, 105
travelling, 108
turning around, 34–5
two-piece mast, 18

universal joint, 11
uphaul, 12
uphauling, 75
upside-down jump, 86
upwind, 39–41

volume, 12, 16, 47, 75

warm up, 112, 117
water start, 14, 16, 61–5
    light wind waterstart, 68–9
    clew first waterstart, 72
wave performance, 96
waves, 82–2, 86–8
weight, 13
weight training, 115–16
wetsuit, 21–2
    care of, 45, 109
wind, 27
wind force, 19, 123
window, 12
Windsurfer (the), 11
windsurfing schools, 23

Learning Resources
Centre